Praise

'Ideas and concept are fantastic.'
— **Lucy,** parent

'WOW, WOW, WOW! BRILLIANTLY written.
Thought-provoking. Challenging. Profound. So easy
to read and left me wanting more!'
— **Camilla,** Occupational Therapy
Professional Lead

'I had been concerned that it might be full of jargon
I wouldn't understand but I quickly realised this
wasn't the case and that it would be understandable
and therefore useful... The book is written by
someone living day to day (and sometimes hour to
hour) with a child with additional needs, instead of
an "expert" who has read all the research but has no
idea what it's actually like to have this as your life,
where you can't leave the issues at work when you
go home because the issues are at home.'
— **Lynne,** parent

'... a real wake-up call and a great eye-opener to next
steps for parents and young adults navigating the
future world on offer. It gives direction and support
to those not knowing which way to go.'
— **Scarlett,** parent

'Allows anyone at any stage to believe they can
do it.'
— **Tracy,** parent

What's Possible?

Plan a better future
for your young adult
with additional needs

Graham Caldow

R^{e}think

First published in Great Britain in 2023
by Rethink Press (www.rethinkpress.com)

This book is dedicated to Debra for being a solid rock of loving wisdom in my life. Thank you for believing in me when I didn't. This book wouldn't have been possible without your support and love. Many of the ideas in here have been in partnership – discussed, refined, and reworked to suit our situation – before I felt able to share them.

Contents

Introduction   1

1 The Planned Life   9

  Why our young adults need a life plan   10
  The benefits of a written plan   13
  The Red Giraffe Route Map™   15
  The VOCAL Method™   19
  A planned life in context   23

2 The Daily Living Line   25

  Vision   27
  Options   34
  Create   38
  Assess   49
  Legacy   53
  The Daily Living line in context   57

3 The Relationships Line   61

  Vision   63

Options 70

Create 75

Assess 85

Legacy 91

The Relationships line in context 94

4 The Purpose Line **97**

Vision 99

Options 105

Create 112

Assess 118

Legacy 123

The Purpose line in context 127

5 The Financial Line **131**

Vision 132

Options 139

Create 148

Assess 155

Legacy 161

The Financial line in context 165

Conclusion **167**

References **173**

Acknowledgements **175**

The Author **177**

Introduction

Imagine if your adult child did more around the home. If they had better relationships with people in their life. If they had a purpose to their day, even after full-time education ends. If they began to think about money and how it should be spent. Just think how transformed their future would be, and yours.

It is possible! It's possible if you do what you already do but with more focus and more intention – if you develop a life plan. This book will show you how to make a life plan and how to support your child, or a child for whom you have parental responsibilities, to learn independence skills, manage relationships better, find a purpose to their day, and organise their finances.

We all worry about our children's futures, but as a parent to a child with additional needs, the fears are much more intense. When I use the word parent in this book, it really means anyone who has taken on that role of caring for a young person with additional needs, whether you be a grandparent, sibling, family member or family friend. When my daughter was at school, my priority was often just getting her through the day, through the week. As she grew older, the concerns magnified. I knew she should be taking on more responsibilities around the house and learning skills that might lead to greater independence, but who wants to do that? I knew she should have less screen time, but reducing this is hard with any teenager or young adult, let alone one with additional needs. They have fewer opportunities for leisure activities and often find it difficult to make friends. I worried about her ability to care for and protect herself, and I could see her grasping the mechanics of spending money, but not the concept of the value of money itself. I couldn't see how she could hold down a job, but I was equally concerned about the alternative. How would she hold onto a sense of her own worth when the wider world so frequently undervalued her?

I wondered what would happen to her when I was no longer around to support her. I feared that the life she's been accustomed to would suddenly be taken away, and she would be sent to live somewhere she didn't want to go. I know she likes people in her life, but I have often needed to help her manage relationships with others. It felt important that this emotional need for connection with people was not ignored simply because her mother or I were not around. I was left desperately wanting our daughter to be happy and safe in a world I had learned not to trust because I had become battle-hardened through her school years. I tossed and turned each night, so stressed about a future that I couldn't quite picture. I felt so lost and afraid; perhaps you have too.

My answer was simply to stop worrying about the things she couldn't do, and instead ask myself, what's possible? I drew on my parenting, business and life experience to find a positive answer. With my wife, Debra, we started to look for a better future. We asked ourselves what things our daughter would do easily, what things she would struggle with, and what things she would possibly never be able to do.

We then realised we needed a Vision for different aspects of her life; we needed to decide which Options would work, and then Create a plan; finally, we would need to Assess how well it was working. Once we had clarified all of this, we would have left our Legacy in the way she lives her life on her terms. The anagram formed by this thought process was VOCAL.

We began to put our daughter's life plan into action. Now she does more around the house, she cooks her own meals, and she irons her shirts for work. Outside the house she travels independently on the bus, she goes to cafés on her own, and she shops with friends. She is learning how to deal with customers and work colleagues. She plans her calendar, checks her steps on her watch, and takes our dog for a walk. Each Sunday she does her accounts and tracks her spending during the week. While there is always more to learn, she is well on the way to living semi-independently, and hopefully fully independently in the longer term.

We love our children unconditionally – everyone does. We want them to have a happy, fulfilled life that has dignity, friends and a purpose. As a parent of a child with additional needs, our hopes are no different. Even if there are additional challenges – and sadly our children will face a harder journey than others might – our children also deserve to live their best lives. The best way to bring this about is to plan it, and that has become my purpose: to support others to plan a better life for their children. The aim is to get every young person to achieve their full potential. Do not compare them to other people: success should be measured by whether they do what's possible for them.

The strategies I use form the core of this book. The process we need to undertake with our children can be likened to a train journey. We would not dream of taking a train without first making sure it's heading in the right direction, and so it should be with our children. The framework is the Red Giraffe Route Map™ and the VOCAL Method™. My daughter's favourite colour is red, and her favourite animal is a giraffe – combine them and you get Red Giraffe.

Chapter One gives an overview of why we need a life plan for our children with additional needs. The structure of the plan is straightforward. The Red Giraffe Route Map is divided into four lines, each focusing on a major life area: Daily Living, Relationships, Purpose and Financial. Each line has several stops, and we apply the VOCAL Method at each stop along the line.

Chapter Two focuses on the Daily Living line. This considers the life skills they need to become more independent. This ranges from personal care to household tasks to independent travel. These are the sort of things schools and professional support concentrate on, but rather than focusing on how to teach the skills, our objective is getting your child ready to do more independently.

Chapter Three focuses on the Relationships line. This chapter shows you how to think about managing relationships, both dynamic and static. Dynamic relationships change over time and are with you, family, and friends – people constantly in their life. Relationships with strangers and people they see occasionally are more static. This chapter will help you rethink your relationship with your child and understand how it will change over time and through different life cycles. It's the people in our lives who promote good mental health and give us a sense that our life matters.

Chapter Four focuses on the Purpose line. This chapter shows you how to think about finding an activity – a purpose – after full-time education finishes. This requires actively planning for the next stage of their life and working out what needs to happen for them to progress. The end goal is paid work or a fulfilling voluntary role because purpose can boost our self-esteem and give us an identity.

Chapter Five focuses on the Financial line. This chapter shows you how to think about organising their finances so that they have enough money to live the life you and they wish for. How that should happen varies from person to person, but everyone should have a basic plan for managing income and expenditure. The more control your child has over their own money, the more they will feel encouraged to manage their own life.

Towards the end of each chapter, there is a little about my family's story. I also include four case studies, all loosely based on people I know, but with plenty of artistic licence:

- Ryan has left full-time education and lives with ageing parents.

- Marshall lives in the city with his divorced mother. His father is still active in his life, and his parents try to work together to support him.

- Dana lives with her mother because her father left soon after her birth. They don't have a family support network nearby.

- Kiara has a high-achieving older sister and successful parents. Her parents are struggling with her growing desire for independence.

The main text is full of practical, easy-to-implement ideas to help you explore what's possible for your young adult and plan a better future. The aim is to support them to live the life they want, both now and in the future. I have also provided several free downloads, linked throughout the book, to fast-track the process of devising a life plan. This book aims to support you to build the best possible future for your child, whatever that might be.

ONE

The Planned Life

I t's difficult being a parent to a child with additional needs. Services are often difficult to access, with long waiting lists, and we don't always get the support our children need from healthcare professionals, schools, or the community. Certainly, I often felt overwhelmed in the beginning, and sometimes still do. This can leave us feeling isolated, alone in a world that at times seems determined not to understand or support us.

Undoubtedly, having my daughter has made me a better person, although admittedly maybe the benchmark wasn't that high to begin with! If we're honest with ourselves, however, most of us would not have chosen this journey for our child. It is tough, frustrating, demoralising, and lonely. I have certainly learned to give more and be less selfish, and I'm sure you have too. For what you've already been through, you have my respect. I don't know you personally, or your story, but there are similarities in all our stories.

We live in a world where other parents don't appreciate, let alone understand, our struggles and fears. We need to recognise that we do face unique challenges, and it's not wrong to want support and assistance from those in our community and healthcare providers. In short, as parents, we often feel frustrated. We live with guilt, even when uncalled for, and we are tired: tired of teaching skills that are quickly forgotten, tired of explaining things that sometimes seem obvious, both to our children and to others, and tired of battling a system that often seems set up to fight against us, rather than to support us and our child. Sometimes it is hard to imagine a future in which everything works out just fine for our children, where they have friends, do something with their day, and have a sense of dignity. However tough it feels, we owe it to our children to put our fears aside to help them build a better future.

Why our young adults need a life plan

Have you ever woken up in the morning and thought, 'My life hasn't turned out the way I expected'? But you also know that despite this, you've been able to make the best of the situation and it's turned out OK.

However, our young adults are not usually so adaptable, and the ramifications of living an unplanned life could be devastating.

For many years, I didn't have a plan for my daughter. I had a vague notion of trusting the education system and hoping for the best. I saw teachers, occupational therapists, and speech and language therapists make a difference in her development, even though she continued to fall behind her peers, but as the end of full-time education loomed, I couldn't imagine her having the skills she needed to live the life she wanted without me around to support her.

I realised that my daughter needed a holistic life plan. We, as a family, needed clarity on what she actually wanted in her life and from life. We needed to identify goals, priorities and values. This would help us focus on what really mattered so that we wouldn't get distracted, and it would be easier to evaluate different options and choose the ones that best align with our goals. It would also motivate us by reminding us of what was most important because a life plan makes us accountable for our own success. It helps us to take ownership and control of the choices we make.

Debra and I had to do something we had not done with our own lives – identify a long-term plan with short- and medium-term priorities. We needed to consider what we wanted the year 2050 to look like for our daughter, but also to think deeply about what the next year might bring, and then the next three, five and ten years. Establishing this vision enabled us to simplify and focus our efforts, otherwise the objective of achieving greater independence might seem too big to accomplish. We needed to break down each goal into smaller, actionable steps (or 'stops') to move us closer to our overall goal. This became the Red Giraffe Route Map.

As part of this process, in 2017, Debra started the Journey Skills podcast, because we saw this as a journey that we needed to undertake if we were to equip our daughter with the skills she needed to live her life to its fullest. Later the podcast changed its name to Expanding Worlds because many of the themes related to expanding the horizon of what's possible for our young adults. It is about sharing stories, solutions and successes. The podcast is still going strong and can be found at www.expandingworlds.com.

After we set our direction, we needed to be able to assess progress. We wanted to ensure we reviewed our goals regularly to make sure we were heading in the right direction. That is not to say we shouldn't adjust as necessary along the way – we knew our goals and priorities would change over time, especially as what's possible changes as both our daughter and the world develop. Our life plan therefore needed to be able to reflect new options and changes of opinion and incorporate them as necessary. We also had to remember to celebrate successes along the way.

Above all, we needed to remember that writing a life plan is a personal process, and there isn't a one-size-fits-all approach. Over the last twenty years, we have learned to do things differently, and we shall continue to do so. We wanted to take time to reflect on what was important for us, not what everyone else does. For too long we did not have an answer, but working through this process eventually enabled us to clarify our vision. I hope this book will inspire and support others to start planning earlier than I did.

The benefits of a written plan

There are three major benefits to a written plan. The first is to avoid regrets. When our children are born, we are full of enthusiasm for teaching them about the world and how to live in it. When our children have additional needs, we may find this often yields little progress and we become frustrated and disappointed somewhere along the way. We lose some of our teaching energy and ambition, but it is our children who lose out. They don't learn to do the things that would give them more freedom and control over their lives, because we are tired and find it quicker, easier, and less hassle to do it ourselves. In the long term, they may struggle when we are no longer around to support them. We cannot find a way to defy the laws of nature and the ageing process, so instead we must somehow overcome our frustrations and find the energy to start again, but this time in a smarter way and with a life plan. The worst thing we can do is let our own weaknesses and limitations hold us captive as this will lead to our fears of our children being left alone, vulnerable in the world, coming true.

The second benefit is to provide clarity and filter opportunities. We know *who* matters most but not always *what*. Often we don't know how to make a life plan, or we think making one will be too hard, excessively long, or just a little bit too scary. However intimidating it might seem, the cost of *not* having a life plan will be greater because we won't prioritise what is most important, nor base decisions around this because we don't know what we want to achieve. Michael Hyatt and Daniel Harkavy, authors of *Living Forward: A proven plan to stop drifting and get the life you want*, suggest that a life plan provides clarity on what needs to be done so that we naturally focus on what's most important to us. It outlines our priorities and filters opportunities to ensure we always do what matters most.

The third benefit of a written plan is to help us face reality. This can be incredibly difficult because we like to think that somehow it will all turn out alright. We hope luck will smile on our children, but there is always that thought at the back of our mind, *will it?* We try to ignore the perils of our child's situation because they are safe now, while they are with us, but the reality is that if we don't face the truth, however challenging, our children will not be able to live a full life, filled with stimulating activity and a sense of achievement. The consequence is an underprepared and unskilled child, lacking in self-esteem and self-value, confused in a world they don't understand, and secretly feeling that they aren't worth much because they can't do much. If, however, we confront our challenges head-on, we can, with effort, imagine a different reality, a better destination. There is no reason why they can't have a great future in which they are safe, happy, and have a real sense of self-worth, but we need to be active in the process to make it happen.

It is important to emphasise that a life plan doesn't need to be long. It only needs to be a few pages, most of which are mapped out for you in the bonus handouts that accompany this book. As an added resource, there's also a copy of the life plan I've created with and for my daughter.

The Red Giraffe Route Map™

The problems you currently face are those we also faced as a family. We developed a way to make a life plan for our daughter and our life plan will work for you too. We created the Red Giraffe Route Map by dividing the main aspects of her life into four categories which we liken to train lines. The diagram below is simplified; later chapters will expand the number of stops on each line and propose some strategies you can use at each stop, but for now, let's keep it simple.

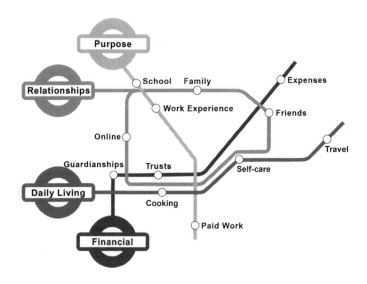

The Red Giraffe Route Map™

The first of the four lines is the Daily Living line. This relates to the everyday living skills your sons and daughters need to live their daily lives both inside and outside the home and to look after themselves. Along the line are several stops: each stop is something that you feel needs to be addressed in your life plan for your child. In this simplified example, you can see three specific stops: Cooking (which relates to food preparation in general, because everyone needs this skill to some degree), Self-care and Travel; your route map will list several more.

As you and the people in your life grow over time, relationships develop and change; for this reason, the second of the lines, the Relationships line, is circular. To ignore relationships in a life plan would be to ignore the importance people play in our everyday lives and our feelings of connection to the world and society. Our young adults need this as much as anyone else, even if they don't always enjoy interacting with others. Relationships with Family and Friends often require additional work, and sometimes online friends become a chief source of companionship; these online friendships need a specific strategy, and so Online is regarded as a separate stop. The Relationships line recognises that feelings of loneliness can be the worst part of the human condition, and thus we need to plan which people will be in their lives and how that will happen.

The Purpose line is to ensure our young adults have some sort of occupation, and here it is especially important to have a plan. It's easy for them to fall out of engagement with the world and end up with nothing to do but stay at home all day. Even school – despite its challenges, and with the annoying 'boss' at the front of the class (the teacher) – is a reason to get out of bed in the morning. Without such a reason, it's all too easy to become isolated and suffer from a lack of purpose. Regardless of the somewhat disheartening employment statistics for young adults with additional needs – in England only 5.1% of adults known to their local authority have paid work[1] – it is crucially important to put this as a central part of their

---

1   Mencap, www.mencap.org.uk/learning-disability-explained/
     research-and-statistics/employment-research-and-statistics, accessed
     July 2023

life plan, if for no other reason than to ensure good mental health. Work Experience may be a stop along the way, but the end goal needs to be either Paid Work (even if only on a part-time basis) or a community volunteering role of some kind. The emphasis shouldn't be only on the money they might receive, but rather on the self-esteem and sense of identity it gives them.

Having devised a plan to allow them to live with more independence, manage their relationships, and have a purpose to fill a good part of their day, this would all go to waste if their finances aren't organised. Guardianships is a stop some might not think is for them, but it is an important stop for many. It may be that you choose to put more reliance on Trusts and therefore you will focus more heavily on this stop, as well as teaching them how to manage their expenses.

Each of us will have different stops on the Financial line, depending on your child's ability to manage money, but for everyone, this is about organising their money in a way that enables them to continue to live the life you have given them the ability to live, without the fear of homelessness or extreme poverty. To ensure this, it is imperative that their finances are planned in the same way as the other major parts of their life.

While these four lines cannot cover every conceivable aspect of their life, they do cover all the major components. A plan for each of these will protect them in a way we will not always be able to and will give them a happy life they enjoy living.

The VOCAL Method™

Having established our plan, we now need a method to implement and teach our children the things they need to know. The process we used with our daughter gave us the acronym VOCAL. When used with the Red Giraffe Route Map, the VOCAL Method will help you support your children to learn the skills they need to become more independent.

The VOCAL Method is a five-step approach that breaks down the implementation and teaching process and enables us to refine a Vision, evaluate Options, Create a plan, Assess their progress, and finally, deliver a Legacy.

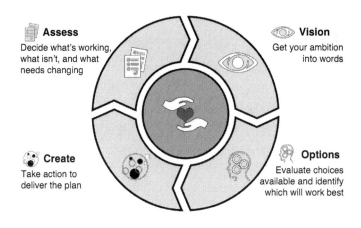

Assess
Decide what's working, what isn't, and what needs changing

Vision
Get your ambition into words

Create
Take action to deliver the plan

Options
Evaluate choices available and identify which will work best

The VOCAL Method™

V: Vision

Vision is picturing how the future will look. We need an overall vision for each line as well as for each stop on that line. It is about being ambitious and asking what's possible. It is about having goals and a general direction to aim towards, even if the vision gets rerouted along our journey.

Sometimes getting started is the hardest thing. We don't need all the answers to start, but we do need to start to find the answers. A vision is a logical place to begin, even if it is not fully thought through. This means questioning what your child wants to be able to do in the future, preferably via an open active discussion with them. This then allows their thoughts and ours to be aligned and focused in the same general direction. Once we have that direction, we can think about the things that need to happen to make that vision a reality.

O: Options

After we picture a vision, we need to identify some options for each stop. This is the time when you fully evaluate the choices available to your child to identify what might work best. It is about deciding what will work for your child, given their individual strengths and limitations. Sometimes this may mean thinking about your child's background and evaluating any constraints there might be. Included in this, you need to identify where they are now as the starting point.

C: Create

Create is putting in place the plans needed to implement whichever options you have identified are right for your child. This is a process of *doing* rather than *talking about doing*. It's not about the speed of progress, but rather about ensuring progress is being made in the general direction. This is about taking action to deliver on the plan so that, over time, it becomes a reality.

A: Assess

After action has been taken and time allowed for progression, plans need to be assessed. It is here that you decide what is working well, what is not, and what needs adapting or changing. You may decide to go round to Options or Create again to make adjustments, or you may decide you have reached what you feel is a successful outcome.

L: Legacy

Legacy is often narrowly understood as 'things left to someone in a will', but we prefer to consider the term more broadly. Maybe you can think of someone in your community that's credited with making things better, improving local services, or being an example to learn from; this is their legacy.

Our interpretation of legacy is similar. It's about delivering on your vision for your child; it's giving them the ability to do things for themselves. As the proverb says, 'Give a person a fish and you feed them for a day; teach them to fish and you feed them for a lifetime.' Legacy is when you can tick off a stop on a line, knowing that they now have that skill to use for the rest of their life. In effect, your legacy is something you give them before you leave them.

OUR STORY: The day my second daughter was born

On a November morning almost two years to the day after the birth of our first daughter, we found ourselves looking at the midwife in confusion. She had been checking over our second daughter and had then suddenly called for a doctor.

'Just a precaution,' she said, but we immediately knew something was wrong because the paediatrician came very quickly. The room then filled with people, conversations continued and finally ended with 'SCBU', the special care baby unit, a term unknown to us at the time.

A commotion followed as our tiny baby was taken away, and we looked at each other in confusion as the door closed behind her. The next time we saw our daughter, it was through a plastic incubator in SCBU.

Our life had changed in an instant, even if I didn't realise it at the time. Whatever plans we might have had were swept away. Our daughter would need all the strength we had, and we would have to face challenges and obstacles we could never have imagined.

A planned life in context

Experience has taught us that raising a child with additional needs is challenging, and moving them through the transition to adulthood isn't any easier. To make this transition smoother and to provide them with long-term safety, we need to have a life plan. This life plan needs to be tailored to your child, their needs and their aspirations, and it should identify everything important to them, first and foremost, as well as to you.

The Red Giraffe Route Map is a blueprint to help establish those key priorities, as well as the other things that must be carefully thought about. It is a way of breaking down our overall goals for a particular aspect of their life into smaller steps to be accomplished – our stops along the lines. It is designed and conceived specifically to support families who want to enable their young adults to live more independently. It is a plan that not only considers the physical aspects of daily living, but also deals with the emotional and psychological aspects of their mental wellbeing, including their relationships, and ensuring they have a purpose to their day. To underpin this, it also addresses financial concerns.

The VOCAL Method is a way to structure our efforts to accomplish each stop on their route. It's a way to make sure that their life plan becomes reality, by identifying their goals, deciding on the best option to achieve these, creating a plan to take them there, and assessing how well they are doing. The point of the plan is to deliver your legacy to them in the form of a way of living that works for them now and when you're not around.

The following chapters will go through each of the four lines in turn, showing you how to design and implement a life plan for your child. The point of this book is to assist you in establishing a broad vision for every major area of their life, so you can be direction-ally correct with the decisions you make as your child grows, develops, and matures. Drawing up a life plan can be a difficult process, but the result is liberating and fulfilling, for both you and your child.

TWO

The Daily Living Line

The Daily Living line doesn't usually feature on a more conventional life plan because it's about skills and ways of doing things that most people do with little or no instruction, things like home skills, organising themselves, hygiene, and travel. These life skills don't always come so easily to our children with additional needs, so this line focuses on teaching these things to your child.

By being able to do more of these things for themselves, they will feel more independent and more in control of their own lives, and this will give them a sense of achievement. As they come to master more skills, this may prompt and encourage them to try to do other things as their confidence grows and their abilities expand. By successfully accomplishing these things, they will feel a greater sense of self-worth because of their growing independence.

The Daily Living line considers the things that you already do to help, support, and teach your child, but here with what might be a slightly different emphasis. We shall introduce a number of theories and approaches, some of which you may already be using, along with ideas for embedding these through learning, repetition, and practice. Knowing how to do something is not the same as doing it, and that's where habit comes in.

Thinking about the Daily Living line now allows you to decide how your child will live in the future. Their ability to do home skills will determine to a large extent what type of accommodation will be suitable: the more they can do for themselves, the more likely they are to be able to live independently with minimal support. While this may not be possible for everyone, being able to do more for themselves will allow your child to live with more autonomy within whatever type of accommodation is right for them. After all, there will hopefully come a time when they outlive you, and years of their life will be spent without you around to offer support. Their quality of life may depend on mastering these key skills.

Although we will consider the Daily Living line in isolation, it is important to recognise that it affects all other areas of the life plan. Relationships with others become easier the more your child can do for themselves. No-one likes someone else controlling their every waking moment, and while they probably want the safety you provide, this needs to be balanced against their feeling of autonomy and control over their own life if you are to maintain a healthy relationship with your child. A greater ability to care for themselves will also enhance their relationship with siblings and any other family involved in their care.

When they find a Purpose in their life after full-time education, the ability to perform basic tasks like making coffee or cleaning a workspace will be invaluable, and on the Financial line, personal organisation precedes many of the skills required to manage their money.

Vision

You should be bold and think about what would be possible for your child. You will need to break down the Daily Living line into several stops and have an idea about how each stop will be accomplished. Ask yourself the following question: What could my young adult be doing for themselves in three, five, or ten years?

We should be filling our heads with colourful and exciting pictures so that we can, in turn, enrich our children's heads with these images. We need to ensure that our child knows and really understands the vision as it is only when we have these in mind that we know what to aim for. This sets the direction, even if we don't quite know how to get there.

This visualisation process works for all abilities because there is no right or wrong, nor is there a fixed standard everyone should get to. The only expectation is that your child will be doing a little more than they are now, and that is progress.

On your route map, you may decide to have more or fewer stops, but the point is you should think about what stops your child needs. The diagram below shows examples of some stops.

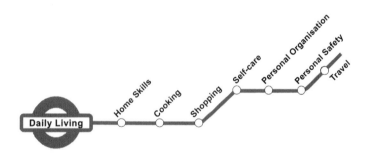

Stops on The Daily Living line

- **Home Skills** encompass household chores, such as cleaning the kitchen surfaces, loading the dishwasher, doing the laundry, and taking out rubbish and recycling.

- **Cooking** ranges from functional food preparation and microwave meals for one to more complicated recipes.

- **Shopping** is something we all do, whether it's buying a single item or weekly groceries. Everyone needs this skill to some degree, including knowing how and when to pay for goods.

- **Self-care** is about tending to one's own needs including personal hygiene, good health and accessing appropriate medical care, getting a good night's sleep, and deciding upon a healthy and balanced diet.

- **Personal Organisation** can include tasks such as making lists for shopping, to-do lists, making and keeping track of appointments, or planning the next day.

- **Personal Safety** is relevant to everyone to some degree, whether that is taking reasonable precautions around sharp objects or locking doors at night. The level of personal safety needed depends upon the intended level of independence, but it includes not sharing personal information, being aware of their surroundings and deciding how to manage certain situations.

- **Travel** marks a certain level of independence. Not everyone will be able to drive or afford a car so they may need to navigate public transport. This will require an understanding of timetables, when and from where a bus or train leaves, and what to do if the bus or train is cancelled.

What would you call success?

You should decide what level of skill you want your child to achieve at each stop. This is important because it is easy to expect too much of them or, even more dangerously, expect too little. We want what's possible, nothing more, nothing less. Do not be distracted by what others can do. You should define success as your child reaching *their* full potential. This distinction is important. Each of our children has their own unique capabilities, and it is unfair to compare them.

Depending on their abilities, consider the following possible short-term manifestations of success:

- **Home Skills:** Success might be taking their plate to the kitchen, or for someone else, it might mean loading and unloading the dishwasher, vacuuming their room each week, keeping their clothes tidy, or changing their bed sheets.

- **Cooking:** Success might be making a sandwich for lunch or cooking a family meal once a week; it may also mean planning and cooking their meals, Monday to Friday.

- **Shopping:** Success might be going to the cashier to pay for a single item, or taking a basket of groceries through the self-checkout.

- **Self-care:** Going to the bathroom when needed, getting dressed on their own or brushing their teeth are all examples of successful self-care; it may also mean managing their stress levels by using a card system to show their feelings, taking a deep breath before reacting, or counting to ten.

- **Personal Organisation:** Here success might be basic time management, packing their bag in the evening for the next day, using online calendars to plan the upcoming week, or creating reminder alarms.

- **Personal Safety:** Success might be knowing when to ask for help, or it might mean knowing what precautions to take when home alone.

- **Travel:** Success here might mean crossing the road safely or taking a bus across town; the final triumph might include coping well when travel plans and schedules are interrupted by unexpected events, such as a cancelled train.

The point is that success will be different for each of our young people, and their successes should be acknowledged and celebrated as such.

RYAN'S STORY

Since leaving college, Ryan has not been able to find anything to do with his level 1 qualifications. He spends most of his time sitting at home. His parents don't stop him watching the screen because they are exhausted and they just want him to be happy. They can't imagine him ever living away from them.

Then things suddenly changed. His father developed a problem with his heart and was rushed to hospital by ambulance. His condition soon stabilised, but both he and Ryan's mother were totally unprepared to be told that he needed to take early retirement. His job was too physical, and he needed significant time and complete rest to recover. Their plans hadn't accounted for this, nor had their finances.

Ryan's mother realises that she can't do everything anymore, especially as she also now has to care for her husband. She explains to Ryan that, out of necessity, he will have to start helping around the home. She starts thinking about all the skills she wants him to be able to do and that she thinks he can take on. His first tasks are home skills. He takes plates to the kitchen and washes them. At first, they didn't come up as clean as his mother wants, but gradually, with practice, he gets better. Cooking wasn't on his radar because his mother always did it, but with his father's health scare, Ryan needs to learn. Over the following month, he makes progress and gradually takes on more tasks and learns new skills.

There are also other changes in Ryan, things his mother had not expected. As he does more around the house, he feels more and more like a contributing member of the family, a key part of Team Help Dad Recover. His confidence grows and he starts taking on additional tasks without being asked as his sense of self-worth increases.

His mother wondered why it took such a dramatic event for them to get Ryan's life into focus. She wished they'd started this earlier as she sees her son blossoming.

Actions for Vision

The aim of this book is to help you to write an overarching life plan for your child. Initially, it is something you may write to get your thoughts about their life clarified and organised, but with time, and for it to be effective, your child should have input into it. Your first life plan draft can be written as you go through this book, one bit at a time.

To get started, you need to decide which stops on the Daily Living line are necessary for your child. Most people follow the same stops, but you will personalise your life plan. This may mean you include more stops or fewer; it doesn't matter so long as it works for you.

Visit www.whatspossibleplan.com/resources for the free bonuses that come with this book, including a download to use when deciding on your stops on the Daily Living line. If you use the list of stops as a starting point, this exercise should not take very long.

Options

When thinking about options for individual stops – what is and isn't possible – we need to consider what hasn't worked in the past. Sometimes there are physical constraints; other times it has been because we haven't identified the right option or implemented it consistently.

Physical constraints come in many forms. My daughter does not have a great deal of upper body strength and sometimes this limits her. To address this, we have needed to think about aids that can help, such as jar openers and easy grip utensils. We also bought an air fryer so she could avoid taking heavy trays from a hot oven.

Sometimes past failures may have been due to a lack of planning on our part rather than a physical or other constraint. For example, we had repeated complaints when our daughter's favourite hoodie wasn't clean. This made us think about our options, and we decided to buy her a laundry basket for her room. We agreed that she would bring her laundry downstairs to the machine on specific days of the week, and her clothes were washed separately. This removed blame from us if the hoodie wasn't clean because only those clothes brought down got washed, and it also taught her something about personal responsibility. As a next step, it was natural to get her to start loading the machine, show her exactly how to turn it on, and then make it her job to hang out her clothes.

Sometimes options have not worked because of a lack of consistent implementation. I have on occasion been guilty of doing things for my daughter because it was quicker and easier for me. This meant my daughter didn't get to consolidate a skill because of a lack of opportunity for her to practise, so it never became an ingrained and easy habit. If she couldn't do something and I didn't let her practise, it wasn't her fault if her abilities didn't improve.

There will be times when we will have to imagine a whole new way of doing something at a particular stop. This is when technology can be an asset. For example, we have a robotic vacuum cleaner for our house. It is small, light, and easy to empty, so enabling our daughter to vacuum her room is simple; in fact, she doesn't mind putting it on in the rest of the house either (it may also be that it's the tech she likes…).

Options for stops vary for each of us, depending on what constraints we have, but you know your child better than anyone else. As Malcolm Gladwell argues in *Outliers: The story of success*, if we spend at least 10,000 hours practising something then we become experts. There is no doubt you've clocked up well over 10,000 hours caring for and learning about your child by the time they've become a young adult, so you are undoubtedly the expert on them. The thing you need to do now is to use that expertise in your planning.

You should also bear in mind that options change over time, as your child grows up and begins to mature. This gives them a greater understanding of rewards and consequences, and things you thought were impossible become possible. This may then open up new options to learn new skills.

Housing options

Few people live in the same place their whole lives. Living in a warm, safe, and secure place is something we all want for ourselves, and we want this for our children too. It is likely that they will live away from you eventually, if only because they outlive you, so it makes sense to begin to think about housing options well in advance.

Depending on where you live, there may be organisations providing a housing solution that could work for your child. Options for housing are sometimes explored on the Expanding Worlds podcast. For example, in Episode 114 we featured an organisation called *Main Street* where young people live in a purpose-built apartment block alongside other members of their local community. Other examples include *US Autism Homes*, featured in Episode 120, and *My Stomping Ground*, featured in Episode 121.

If there are organisations like these in your local area, you should contact them early to find out if they have a waiting list and how their application process works. Even if there are no similar options locally, these are great examples of parents working together to build genuinely inclusive solutions that focus on developing a community around and for our young adults, and they might inspire you to seek out – or set up – something similar.

MARSHALL'S STORY

Marshall is fifteen and lives in the city with his mother, who is divorced. His father is still around and active in Marshall's life, although he lives with his second wife. Because of Marshall's emotional needs, his parents haven't planned for him to live fully independently, so their stated aim is supported accommodation. However, his mother sometimes feels Marshall may be able to do more than they think.

To address some immediate concerns, his parents decide they want to work on Marshall's travel skills. He already has some travel skills, and he can cross the road by himself and often goes to the local shop alone, so they begin to wonder whether he can travel independently from his mother's apartment to his father's and back again. They look at the options and discover there is a direct bus that runs between their homes.

Marshall is physically large for his age but finds some social situations difficult, which makes his parents think he might be vulnerable when he's on public transport, despite his size. To address this, when they talk about how he might make the journey, they discuss with him why it is a good idea to sit near the driver.

Marshall downloads the bus app. Over time he learns how often the bus comes, and to text each parent about what time he will arrive at their place. He uses Apple Pay for the journey.

Since proving to his parents and himself that he is capable of travelling independently, Marshall's confidence has grown and now he is asking if he can travel into the town centre by himself one day.

Actions for Options

Options is about looking at your vision and considering what's the easiest way to realise it. It doesn't matter how other people do things; it's about how your child can do things. If something becomes easy for them to achieve because of an option you have selected, brilliant! It might be possible to extend the goal for that stop further, particularly with layered skills like cooking. Think about what you want to achieve and ask yourself if there is anything you can use or do to make reaching this particular goal easier. For example, a laminated list of microwave cooking times and chore lists, perhaps placed on your fridge, smart speakers with reminder announcements and phone apps containing routines, and so on.

Create

Once you have decided on the best options for a stop, you need to develop a plan to make progress happen.

How you generate the plan will be individual to you, but at each stop, you should make a list of the necessary steps in the process. Plans for each stop will have different timescales depending on how complex the stop is and how much of it is already completed.

To tick off a stop as accomplished, your child needs to be able to do everything involved and do it consistently. They will need to learn new skills, use repetition so they know the process, and practise it enough so it can be performed in any context. We then need to ingrain this as a habit that is repeated each time. There are several methods and techniques that can be used to assist in this process. This next section is the most theoretical, but these are useful concepts to introduce because they provide context and several suggested strategies to use when establishing new habits in your child.

Scaffolding

Scaffolding is a term used when offering support to learn a new skill. Like a scaffold on a building, scaffolding is a temporary structure that is gradually removed so less support is offered (and needed) as these new skills develop.

How you demonstrate a new skill or behaviour will vary depending on how complex the task is. Complex tasks should be broken down into a series of individual steps so that each step can be demonstrated.

Where possible, you should try to build on what they already know. Then you need to start *fading*, that is, withdrawing support gradually as they become more competent and confident at doing the task themselves. Scaffolding should only be there while they need it.

Once a skill has been learned, it needs repetition to ensure your child remembers what they need to do. When people learn something new, connections form between the neurons in their brain. Those connections are strengthened and reinforced each time they do that activity.

After repeating, the final stage is practice. This is subtly different from repetition, or rote learning. For something to be so ingrained that it happens automatically and without excessive effort, we need to practise it in different contexts, such as at different times or in different environments. For example, think of some of the things you or your child learned at school. You went through the learning and repetition stages, perhaps in preparation for a test or exam, but promptly forgot it all immediately after. This is because the skill was not quite embedded in the practice stage. Consistent practice in different situations would have ingrained it and formed a lasting memory and skill.

Forwards and backwards chaining

Forwards chaining is something you have probably done since your child was very young, but you have not put a name to it. Forwards chaining teaches the steps of the task in order, starting with the first and moving forward until the task is completed. It breaks down complex tasks into manageable steps. To use a food example, making a sandwich: first they are shown how to get all the ingredients ready, such as bread, butter, and cheese. Second, they butter the bread. Third, they put the cheese in the sandwich, and so on for all the other steps, including using a knife to cut the sandwich, until they make lunch for themselves.

While this is a simple example, forwards chaining can be used to show how to do more complex tasks. Forwards chaining is beneficial because it allows them to build up confidence and experience success early on, and this encourages them. By starting with the first step, this process provides them with a clear under-standing of the sequence of steps required to complete a task, which can help them to stay focused and moti-vated in the early stages. As they learn the steps in the right order, forwards chaining is more intuitive and can be particularly useful for children or young adults with sequencing problems.

Backwards chaining is similar, except you teach your child the last step first, and then each step is taught in reverse order until they can do everything for themselves. Like forwards chaining, it offers an immediate reward and sense of achievement as the result is the first step accomplished, and this can be a great motivator and confidence boost for the child or young adult. You might prefer to use backwards chaining over forwards chaining if the task is more complex with many more steps within steps, and the easiest steps to learn are the ones at the end.

To use another food example, when cooking a family meal, you might first identify all the steps involved. Second, you might demonstrate the last step, like how to plate up the food. Third, you would assist and encourage them to do this until they can confidently do it on their own. Fourth, you would show them how to do the steps immediately before serving, repeating each one before introducing the next until they can do all the steps needed. Back chaining encourages them by allowing them to focus on one step at a time, starting with a reward, and gives them an immediate positive feeling of success for each step completed.

Forming habits

It's easy to think that by getting to the practice stage, your child has accomplished a stop. They have learned a skill and practised it so many times and in several different contexts that they have become proficient at it, but there is a little more to it than this. Having the ability to do something is not the same as being motivated to do it if something else seems easier. This means you need to support your child to develop habits.

We might define a habit as a behaviour that is nearly or completely involuntary. According to Charles Duhigg in *The Power of Habit*, habits are the keys to success. They are powerful because they shape our daily lives and long-term outcomes.

Duhigg's Cue-Routine-Reward model is a framework for understanding how habits work. He explains that every habit consists of three components:

- **Cue:** The trigger that initiates the habit. It is the signal that tells the brain to go into automatic mode and start the routine.

- **Routine:** The behaviour or action that is performed in response to the cue. It is the habit itself, the automatic behaviour that is repeated over and over again.

- **Reward:** The positive outcome or reinforcement that the brain receives as a result of performing the routine. It is what makes the brain want to repeat the behaviour in the future.

Duhigg argues that by understanding the Cue-Routine-Reward model, we can identify the cues and rewards that drive our habits, and then choose to change them if we want to. If we want to break a bad habit, we need to identify the cue that triggers it and replace the routine with a different, more positive behaviour that still provides a reward. Alternatively, if we want to form a new habit, we can identify a cue and a reward that aligns with the behaviour we want to adopt until it becomes automatic.

This idea is expanded further by BJ Fogg in *Tiny Habits: Why starting small makes lasting change easy*. He argues that making small, incremental changes through the introduction of tiny achievable habits is the most effective way to build lasting behaviour change. Fogg's argument is based on the principle of behaviour design, which involves identifying the specific behaviours that lead to the desired outcome and then breaking them down into small, achievable steps. He suggests that traditional approaches to behaviour change, such as setting lofty goals or relying on willpower, are often ineffective because they require too much effort and are not sustainable over the long term. In contrast, tiny habits are easy to do, require minimal effort, and can be easily integrated into daily routines. By starting small and focusing on creating new habits that are easy to sustain, Fogg believes people can build momentum and achieve lasting behaviour change.

Fogg makes the point that motivation and ability also play a factor. Once a cue takes place (Fogg prefers the term 'prompt'), whether a person does something or not is also related to how easy it is for them to do and/ or how motivated they are to do it. He emphasises the importance of celebrating even the small wins and feeling good about progress made, which can help to reinforce new habits and build confidence.

Using Fogg's argument, if your child is strongly motivated to do something, or if it is within their ability and does not require much effort, the chances are high that, after being prompted by a cue, they will act and do it. However, if their motivation is low, or they feel they lack the ability to do a task, then it is less likely they will do it. When trying to develop new habits with our children, the key is to identify those tasks which they are either highly motivated to do or are well within their ability. If they lack motivation but can do a task, the reward for developing that habit will need to be strong. If they lack the ability but are highly motivated to do a task, they will want to try to do that task, but you need to find ways to develop their ability.

Another useful tool is habit stacking which, as the name suggests, is where habits are stacked on top of each other. For example, your child could take their plate to the kitchen after every meal. Once that habit is embedded and they do it every time, then they could then move on to taking out everyone's plates; this could then progress to putting the plates in the dishwasher. Each time the habit becomes embedded, you can stack an additional task on top until you get to the point where the whole set has been achieved.

Clearly, in this situation, motivation may be low which means the reward must be strong and should be instant. It can't be a promise to take them bowling at the weekend if something is done every day during the week – Fogg argues that this would be an incentive, not a reward. A reward happens during or immediately after the event, while the dopamine is still flowing, and it can be as small and simple as a fist bump. Anything so long as it is something immediate. The key is that the reward must be experienced immediately after the habit is performed, thus reinforcing the behaviour and making it more likely to be repeated in the future.

Planning for success

While working on the Daily Living line, you will develop many plans because you will need one for each stop. You will need to spend time teaching the steps in the plan, but at some point, you need to establish an unmistakable and memorable cue so that it becomes a habit that gets performed automatically.

More than anything else, the cue must be reliable. You should spend time thinking about how these cues will happen at various times and in different places, and also consider whether there are natural occurrences at various times of the day to which you can attach a cue. For example, finishing the evening meal can be a time-related cue to pack their bag ready for the next day, or a cue might be an alarm set to remind them to take their medication. With consistent use, they will develop a habit of doing these things at a specific time.

You need to teach each skill at the right pace for your child's ability and the complexity of the stop. Some stops can be taught entirely by habit stacking; others need a combination of habit stacking, scaffolding, and either forwards or backwards chaining. Trying to rush this process could delay the development of a lasting habit. For our part, we need to be prepared to take carefully calculated risks, preferably in as controlled a manner as possible, and trust in our children. This is particularly true when it comes to independent travel for the first time. While this needs nerve on our part, if we do not allow them to do certain things, we are holding them back and preventing them from growing – none of us wants to do that.

DANA'S STORY

Dana is nineteen and has lived with her mother since her father left a couple of months after she was born. Her mother does not have a support network nearby, no family close, or anyone she can really rely on.

Dana's mother wants her daughter to develop some independence skills and decides she should buy her own items at the supermarket. Ever since she was a young child, Dana has shopped with her mother. Once she got old enough, she was given responsibility for pushing the trolley.

Dana's mother has decided to take this a step further and asks Dana to get some items and put them in the trolley. At first, it's just items Dana is highly motivated to find – popcorn for Friday home movie night, for example, and the items that Dana can find – the regular staples they shop for each week, such as cereal and bread. Then she starts to get Dana to work through a short shopping list.

Next Dana was given responsibility for scanning items at the self-checkout, and packing the groceries, remembering always to put the heaviest items at the bottom of the bag. Gradually Dana's mother began to stand back as Dana became proficient at scanning and packing.

Because the increase in Dana's responsibility was gradual, she didn't notice that she was now doing almost everything by herself. Dana's mother paid by contactless card but decided that was another part of the process Dana should do. They started going to the supermarket with separate shopping lists. Dana shopped for her personal items and Friday night popcorn and used her own card to pay.

Actions for Create

When you thought about options, you might have thought of a device or trick to make reaching a goal easier to achieve. However, achieving goals generally also requires a strategy or process. You need to think about how you are going to teach your child to do what's required for each stop. Look through your list of stops and decide what strategies or techniques you are going to use. For example, you might use scaffolding at the supermarket, or when teaching them to ride a bike or travel by public transport; forwards chaining might be used to start them making their lunch or loading the dishwasher; backwards chaining might be more suited to cooking a meal or cleaning their teeth.

Teaching a skill is one thing, but learning to do it consistently is another. This is where habit comes in, and we should not underestimate the importance of habit to achieving success. Ask yourself what cue can be used to initiate the habit. There also needs to be a tangible reward for them, even if it's just a positive feeling about accomplishment.

Assess

You need to give the plan time to work, and then you need to assess how well the plan is working. To do this assessment accurately, however, we need to learn how to recognise the difference between a lack of success because more practice is required, compared to a lack of success because something is simply not working. One requires more time; the other requires more thought. At each stop, we should assess whether they are moving forward in terms of learning skills required, even if the stop has not yet been fully accomplished.

Assessing progress

Progress will be obvious to you. The practice stage of learning a new skill will indicate whether they understand how to do a task, and reveals their flexibility and ability to cope if something changes. If it is the sort of task that requires lots of practice in different contexts – cooking, for example – if an occasion arises when an ingredient is not available, you can immediately assess how well they adapt and cope. When first teaching the skill, you would have made calculated decisions about when to take away the scaffolding; whether to give something a little more time to work is harder to assess. Remember that it is not a failure to abandon some tasks because they are not moving forward in favour of looking for other ways to achieve the end result. As Zig Ziglar in *Developing the Qualities of Success* points out, 'failure is an event, not a person.'[2]

A key component to assess at this stage is your child's feelings about *how* you are teaching them. They should feel that the way you help them learn works for them too. Learning works best when it's a positive experience. If it is not, the way you are teaching might need changing or adapting.

Another thing to evaluate is whether habits are being formed in relation to skills. If habits are not being formed, and it is not a case of a lack of ability or motivation, then you must decide whether it's an issue with either or both the cue or the reward. Does the cue need to be changed? Should you anchor the cue to

2   Zig Ziglar, *Developing the Qualities of Success: How to stay motivated* (Made for Success Publishing, 2014)

a different time that fits better within their schedule? The reward, or lack thereof, could also be an issue. Maybe you need to evaluate what they get from doing the task. Put yourself in their position to ask, 'Why would I be bothered to do this?'

Does their future look better?

Progress at individual stops is one thing, but there also needs to be progress over the whole Daily Living line. Achieving this should gradually begin to make a noticeable difference in their life and your family life.

As they make progress, can you see their confidence growing? Are they less frustrated because they feel they have greater control over their life? Have their newly acquired skills opened up more options for developing further skills? Is this in alignment with the vision?

KIARA'S STORY

Kiara is twenty-two and lives in the city with her parents. She has an older sister, who is building a successful career in another city 200 miles away. Her parents have a vision of Kiara living independently by twenty-five, with a flatmate and limited support.

Kiara already prepares her lunch and breakfast; however, the cooking of an evening meal is not going as well. Kiara wants to make herself pasta. Her knife skills are poor, so when she chops the onions, they end up in big chunks and don't cook well. She also struggles to drain the pasta.

Her parents reassess their options for this meal. Their solution is to buy frozen precut onion. They also find a pasta oven-bake recipe, which uses fresh pasta and a bake-in sauce.

Her parents also buy an air fryer. Because it is light and easy to use, Kiara can cook both frozen and fresh food in it. Next to it, they place a laminated sheet with the exact cooking times for all the foods she now cooks.

They trial this for a while, making a few more modifications and adjustments to her recipes, before eventually ending up with ten meal recipes. These recipes form the basis of a two-week menu which, when combined with standardised breakfasts and lunches, means Kiara can prepare food for different meals each night for two weeks.

Just to be safe, they show Kiara how to test the heat-detector alarm in the kitchen. This is put as a task on the calendar each week.

Actions for Assess

In our consideration of the Vision stage, we established that taking that first step to begin was an important element, but also that we need to ensure we are directionally correct from the start. Now you have begun, you have made progress, and time has elapsed, so at this point you should reread your life plan to assess whether your child has reached what you defined as success.

If they have, and there's nothing more to accomplish, then great! Celebrate with them! If not, you should take time to consider if it is a case of more time needed, whether the goal should be refined, or indeed if the parameters of success need to be modified. Sometimes a skill just needs more time to learn and embed through repeated practice in different contexts. Other times, our way of teaching might not be working for our child, or we may not have chosen the best options to make it easier. We may also find that how we have defined success in our vision may not be achievable, so we might need to find an alternative definition to set a realistic outcome. Don't feel defeated: the thing to remember is we have found a way that doesn't work for them, and what we now need to do is to think of another way that *will*.

The Assess stage of the method is the time for reflection. This may be done after a month or after a year, depending on what stop you are working on and what skill is required within that stop. The trick is to have your life plan nearby so you are reminded of your original vision and what you have defined as success.

Legacy

One way or another, we all leave our children a legacy, from the way they understand and look at the world, to how they look after themselves inside the home, in the wider world, and a whole lot of other skills as well. The legacy we should aim to leave is our children having a greater degree of independence than they otherwise would have, had they not had your support.

Success can be ticked off in the stops passed on their journey. A group of tasks around Self-care will give our children privacy and independence in the bathroom. Add to this stops such as Cooking, Shopping, and Personal Safety and they are, in theory, able to live independently with little assistance day to day. These are the smaller elements of your legacy, but they will enable you to think about the larger component: where they will live when you are no longer around to support them.

The more stops they master on the Daily Living line, the more they will feel in control of their own lives. Part of this control is greater independence from us, and not having us tell them what to do all the time. This may also produce greater maturity and confidence, as they recognise their achievements. As their ability to do more increases, the more they will want to do for themselves. All these things will help make them happier in themselves.

They will, of course, remember their journey with you, as they look back at their life in later years. They will remember the things you said, the things you did, and the things you taught them; hopefully in time they will internalise these so they become habits of their own. That is why discussing little parts of their life plan with them, painting a vision of an exciting and fulfilled future so they see themselves living that life, is so important. They must imagine their future life and future self before they can live it.

The point of a life plan is so that they achieve all that's possible for them to achieve and so you know their future is as safe and secure as it can be made. This will then help give you the peace of mind you need and give your children a realistic and achievable vision of a future they can make their own.

OUR STORY: A new way of life

When my second daughter was a young child, our lives were punctuated by lots of hospital appointments. Rather naïvely, I imagined local services would be around to support us, but we quickly found we had to fight to get any of the support that it was so clear she needed. At that time, we didn't know any other parents in our local community who had a child with additional needs. We felt so isolated and abandoned.

Three particular episodes stand out for me from my daughter's years at primary school, each a perfect epitome of the type of struggle we faced day to day.

First, when she was the only girl in the class not to get a birthday party invite. A girl my daughter was friends with was having a party. We kept waiting for the invitation to come – I still remember my daughter being so excited about this party, it was obvious it was being talked about between them – but the invitation never arrived. As the date approached, we realised she hadn't been invited. We didn't understand why but we knew for sure this was the parents' decision. On the day of the party, we made some poor excuse to my daughter about an event we had to go to, to explain why she wouldn't be attending the party. My daughter was confused, but she didn't have the communication skills to ask the questions I couldn't answer.

The second occasion was a teacher who thought bullying could be dismissed as schoolyard banter. My daughter was, for a short period, being bullied. When it was reported to this teacher, their initial response was an undertaking to have a word with the children involved, but they also suggested it would be easier for everyone if this wasn't reported officially because it might look bad on the children's school records. We obviously refused his suggestion, but the clear impression was that the teacher valued preserving the reputation of the other children over my daughter's feelings.

The third event occurred as we looked to the years ahead and my daughter's transition to high school. It was obvious something had to change as school was becoming increasingly difficult for my daughter. It was clear that mainstream schooling couldn't meet her needs, and we knew she needed a placement where she had regular access to therapists and staff trained to support her needs.

When we raised this with her primary school, it was clear they believed a local provision was adequate, even if all reports from the professionals who had assessed my daughter suggested otherwise. What should have been a consensus that my daughter's needs should come first became a battle about who should decide where she went next and what support she needed. Rather than a transition from this school to another more suitable placement, we were forced into removing her from her primary school and into home education.

Home education lasted longer than we all would have liked, but we finally came to an agreement with the education authority. Our daughter was offered a place at a great school, and we count ourselves lucky to have found such a positive setting.

All these incidents reinforced for me that I will spend my life fighting for my daughter against the prejudices and negative perceptions of others, but that's OK because despite all these things, she has risen above them. She has proved all these people wrong, and she has made me the proudest father in the world.

The Daily Living line in context

The reason we should develop a plan for daily living skills is because, one way or another, one day our children will have to live without us. This may be either in fully or partially supported accommodation, or independently. Most parents expect siblings (if they have them) to be supportive of their siblings while also leading their own lives; few want or expect them to be full-time carers.

We therefore need to have a vision about where and how they will live and do things for themselves.

Picturing this will help clarify your priorities for them. Not everything on the Daily Living line needs to be done *well*, much of it only needs to be done well enough to get your child by. It is a matter of coming to understand what success looks like for them and what they need to be able to do in their future lives. Having a life plan helps you define what this reality is by thinking about where they will live in the future, how, and with whom.

To get to this successful outcome, we need to decide on options that work, and then the plan we create needs to be consistently followed. Along the way, we constantly appraise how well things are working, and possibly adjust our methods. Having a vision, narrowing down options, and creating a plan doesn't happen seamlessly. It's a process of trial and error, new ideas and correction. The real goal is to get them to a position where it works – that's your legacy.

Put in this context, the Daily Living line frequently intersects with other lines. If they are to live with other people, they will need to be able to manage tasks around the house in a way that fits in with the people they live with. The more they can do for themselves, the more equal they will feel, and in the workplace, whether voluntary or paid, the more skills they have, the more they will feel able to take on new tasks. Daily Living skills often form the bedrock of work-related tasks, and so the more they can do, the more employable they will be. With the Financial line, the more confidence they have in managing their day, the more confidence they will have about managing their money.

The Daily Living line is central to your child's conception of themselves and their place within the world. The more accomplished and confident they feel about the stops along the way, the more they will feel pride in themselves and value their self-worth. They will feel more independent and they won't rely so heavily on others. This will have a knock-on beneficial effect on their relationship with you, their siblings and family, and friends.

THREE

The Relationships Line

A key component of most life plans is relationships with other people. Most of us, if we are honest, would put good family relations at or near the top of our own life plan, along with friends and community, because it's the people around us that give our life its meaning and value. You are, after all, reading this book for someone you love, not for yourself.

The Relationships line aims to bring order and understanding to our interactions with others so our children and young adults with additional needs can navigate them. The benefit of being able to navigate relationships successfully will have a profound effect on their mental health because it gives their life greater meaning. We don't want them to feel lonely – loneliness has an established link to poor mental health, according to the Mental Health Foundation.[3] We want them to know that their life matters to their friends and family, even if they don't seem to want company or find friendships difficult and stressful.

On the Red Giraffe Route Map, the Relationships line is about the interpersonal connections and interactions with others at both a close level, like family and friends, and at a more distant level, with people who aren't necessarily as familiar. It's about helping them to understand that some relationships are fairly static and don't change much, while others are dynamic, and will change and develop over time. An understanding of this will help them navigate the world better.

As before, this line cannot be considered in isolation. These relationships interact with the Daily Living line in that your child will need to speak to the shop assistant, the bus driver or a medical professional. On the Purpose line, they need to communicate and have an ongoing relationship with work colleagues and possibly the public. On the Financial line, they may need to communicate with a bank or utility provider. Of course, for each of these they may have a supportive mentor, but the more they can do for themselves, the better they will feel about themselves, so to get to this point, we need to carve out a vision for their future.

---

3   Mental Health Foundation, 'Loneliness in young people: research briefing', www.mentalhealth.org.uk/our-work/public-engagement/ unlock-loneliness/loneliness-young-people-research-briefing, accessed July 2023

Vision

There are many different types of relationships. Some are easier to navigate than others because they remain largely static; those with family members and friends, for example, are likely to be more dynamic. They involve an ongoing process of reassessment and renegotiation. Sometimes this comes from our child growing and maturing with age; other times it is other people who change. Regardless, the roles people play within these relationships alter over time. Our children need to know how to cope with these changes.

Clearly what is possible differs for each of our children because they have different personalities, interests, and abilities. However, we should picture them in three, five, or ten years, and imagine them managing relationships in a way that works for them but also enables them to get the best out of them.

Over time you might explain to your child that there are different types of people, and our relationships with them will differ. There are people we know well as opposed to people we might only meet once, and then there are people who fall within that divide: people we meet occasionally, like our doctor, and people we spend our time with but who are not close friends. Once they get this idea in their minds, then they might start to think about how they will manage these different relationships in the future.

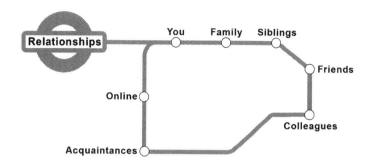

Stops on the Relationships line

While the exact stops on their Relationships line will vary for each of our young adults, some of the key stops will apply to your child:

- **You** are a key relationship in their life.
  This parent-child relationship is a dynamic one that requires reassessment and renegotiation from time to time because it does change. It is unrealistic to expect your child to want the same relationship with you as their knowledge and experience of the world grows. A desire for greater independence, even if it involves a bit of rebellion, is a good thing.

- **Family** might be broken down into grandparents, aunts and uncles, and distant relatives, depending on their significance and presence in your child's life. You may even decide to have a stop for each person.

- **Siblings** (if they have them) might be a single stop or there might be a stop for each sibling.

These are generally lifelong dynamic relationships that evolve and change over time. Both parties will grow as they age, and both will bring new experiences to how they relate to each other.

- **Friends** could be divided into two main types of relationships. There are close friends (although many of our children have difficulty holding down this type of close emotional friendship), which would be a dynamic, changing relationship. You could plan for possible future relationships with partners here, or you may choose to have a separate stop for this. There are also friends they just hang out with (probably most of their school or college friends), and these relationships are probably less dynamic but still changing and evolving. There may also be friends from activities, like sports or social clubs. Friends could be represented by one or more stops, depending on your child.

- **Colleagues** can come from work or voluntary environments. These relationships are usually not static in that they evolve with time and as the environment changes.

- **Acquaintances** are people we encounter occasionally, may sometimes have a brief conversation with, and may then not see again for a while; for example, doctors, dentists, social workers, and other people we know but don't know well. Often the interaction is functional.

- **Online** connections may appear like friends. They are characters in our lives, share their lives and triumphs online and can appear to be part of our life, but often we have never met them, and so don't actually know them, however much we might think we do. It is important to ensure our young adults remain careful about how much they disclose online and remain cautious around these online friendships, however appealing they may seem. Another risk to our children, and one that is perhaps more damaging, is that we see only the edited version of these online friends' lives, lives seemingly filled with status and happiness. The reality is often quite different, and we need to ensure our child understands this.

How you break down the stops is a matter for you and depends on the personality and social skills of your child.

What would you call success?

We need to hold different visions and different definitions of success for different types of people and their interactions. Consider how you might define success in interactions between your child and the following people:

- **You:** Success may be anywhere between them wanting to take the lead more in conversations, to sharing their opinions which you may not agree with. The experience of this might help them learn to manage and challenge other relationships.

- **Family:** Success may be anything between achieving a close and loving relationship with grandparents, to maintaining a distant but polite relationship with other relatives at family occasions.

- **Siblings:** Success in a sibling relationship may be anything from knowing how to have a space to grow in the relationship, to understanding the complex power dynamic that can be managed and changed so that each gets value from the relationship. This relationship will change and evolve throughout their life.

- **Friends:** Success here may be anything between learning how to have close exclusive friendships, just spending time with friends, making small talk in conversations, and adhering to social conventions. It may also be holding down a romantic relationship.

- **Colleagues:** Success in a work setting can be anywhere between being able to converse in a task-related sense, to being able to understand how to move that relationship forward in a professional manner. It may include knowing what not to say as well as what to say.

- **Acquaintances:** Success may be anywhere between understanding the interaction is purely functional to being able to engage in a brief conversation to make the exchange appropriate, pleasant and polite.

- **Online:** Success can be anything from understanding when and what to post online, to knowing the rules and limitations of online friendships.

Success, then, is multiple and varied, depending on who we are talking to and what sort of relationship we have with them. With more static relationships, it is often enough to just know the conventions, a skill much easier to teach than teaching how to negotiate a dynamic relationship successfully.

MARSHALL'S STORY

Marshall's parents separated when he was seven. At the time they told him in simple terms that they still both loved him but they didn't want to be together anymore. As much as his mother wanted to revisit the conversation to explain more, the right time never really came about, but recently Marshall's mother has been thinking about it a lot. She knows in the back of her mind that she needs to reset their relationship so he can have the space to grow into a self-sufficient young man rather than stay a dependent boy.

Before she can get to this, though, the conversation is taken out of her hands. 'Dad's is so much more fun than with you,' he shouted in rage one day, after coming back from his father's place. 'We get takeout and do things. I hate living here!'

She left the room, trying to hide her tears. His words hurt. This wasn't the life she wanted for herself, let alone him, and she felt guilty. Her life hadn't turned out how she had imagined. It took her a few days to get her head around what had happened, but the issue needed confronting. Their relationship, and indeed Marshall's with his father and his father's second wife, needed to be discussed, but how?

She put together a storyboard. It pictured her and Marshall's father before he was born, and a photo of them looking happy and proud as they took him home from the hospital as a newborn baby. She included photos of his life from birth through to now, and even images of what the future might look like. She tried to explain all the love they all had for him in a way he would understand: how they would always love and support him, how he would one day live on his own, and how, one day in the distant future, she and his father would be old and how this was a natural part of life. She presented the storyboard at a time and place that seemed right, but Marshall reacted badly and stormed off. He wasn't ready to hear it.

She looked down at the storyboard, wondering if she should've explained it differently. Then she realised it was him – he might look like a man, but he was still quite immature emotionally. She realised she had to give him time to process this and might need several conversations, using the storyboard and coming back to the same themes time and again. She would have to persevere because some things in life are too important not to talk about.

Actions for Vision

Stops on the Relationships line include family, friends, colleagues, acquaintances, and online. You may decide you want stops for each of your child's siblings, relatives and friendship groups.

Download the bonuses at www.whatspossibleplan. com/resources to decide on your stops on the Relationships line. If you use the list of stops as a starting point, this exercise should not take very long.

You also need to define what success in each of these relationships might look like in your life plan, at least as a starting point for the short term. Defining success for an active, dynamic relationship is a lot harder than defining success with static relationships that are more functional encounters, but start to do this in the relationships section of the download.

Options

When considering options, you should evaluate where your child is now and how you can best support them to improve and enhance their relationships. Sometimes you just want to stop them from making mistakes, as with online relationships. Other times you will want to show them how to participate more and have a broader social circle. This may include being more self-sufficient when dealing with acquaintances and strangers. You may also need options to help them move major relationships in their lives forward, possibly with you or their siblings. The objective is to identify options for what's possible now, but that will also move them a stage further in their confidence and ability because an ongoing relationship will seldom reach an endpoint. This may require some management by you to ensure they are being treated fairly.

Options for online

It seems that there is no other option but to engage online, particularly with social media. To attempt to stop our young adults from using social media is unrealistic and risks them missing out on a big part of everyone else's conversation. The best solution is therefore to think of options to enable them to use social media appropriately and safely, so that it remains beneficial yet, as far as possible, limits its potential negative aspects. This may require a conversation about how others use social media to put it more into perspective. Explain why some people post an edited highlights reel of their lives, and explore why people might choose to ignore the less glamorous or appealing aspects of their own life. Seen from this perspective, characters on social media may lose some of their appeal.

Options for developing confidence

When others speak for us, we feel less engaged with the world. It can be easy to fall into the habit of doing this for our young adults, and they may end up feeling more like a bystander in their own lives. It is therefore important for you to encourage them to take a more active role.

One option could be for them to join clubs or community activities, without you being by their side. Finding opportunities for your child to participate in activities can be a challenge. While your child can be reluctant or scared themselves, sometimes we may find that it is us who are afraid about them not being able to cope, not acting appropriately, or not being able to get past the discomfort of having to speak for themselves. A mistake I made years ago was not wanting my daughter to join a local village club because she was being hassled at school and I thought that would happen at the club. I should have allowed the club organiser the opportunity to be proactive, and this became a lost opportunity for my daughter. What I learned from this was that without risk there is no reward.

Your active relationship management

Close family relationships often need your active management to move them forward. This means you may need to encourage your child to shift the power in their relationship with you. It can be difficult to step out of the shadow of adults and assert independence, but this is exactly what we need to encourage in our young adults for them to become confident enough to express their opinions and beliefs.

We may also find that at times we need to provide a space for personal growth in other relationships as well. Siblings and other relatives are tied by a family connection. Sometimes you might find that family members use language and behave in a way that reflects your young adult when they were a child, not as they are now. This is not good for their self-esteem and reflects these relatives' inability to adapt to the changing relationship. You may need to intervene to remind some people that your child is now a young adult; just like us all, their character, personality and interests have changed and developed as they have grown up. Many families have a relative that doesn't quite understand this.

DANA'S STORY

Dana is approaching the end of full-time education. School was an uphill battle all the way. She was in a special unit at a mainstream school setting. Much of the time she was teased and bullied. She didn't have friends. She couldn't wait to get to college, but things haven't worked out much better there. She still finds it difficult to join a group, even if she does now talk to people in class.

Her mother has agonised over Dana's loneliness. Dana finds it hard to engage because she doesn't ask people those questions that make others feel you are interested in their life. With their lack of family nearby,

Dana and her mother spend a lot of time together, but her mother desperately wants things to change. She wants Dana to have people in her life and for her to enjoy healthy relationships. She also wants her to reduce her use of social media, and move away from the belief that everyone else's life is perfect; she knows how dangerous this is to Dana's view of reality.

Most of all, she wants Dana to feel valued for who she is. She wants Dana to connect with people in a way that's right for her, while keeping herself safe. She knows she cannot stop Dana's social media, especially as she's on it too, but they both agree to turn their phones off at 7.30pm each night. Dana sets an alarm on her phone, so she feels in control of when to say, 'Stop'.

To meet and interact with more people Dana and her mum decide to do a Park Run, a free event held in numerous parks around the world. Dana's mother heard from a friend that Park Run can also be completed as a Park Walk, and this sounded perfect for them. Neither were particularly fit and, as her friend also explained, the event is a social club as much as anything else. Dana's mother hopes that over time Dana might even start to say hello to people she sees each week.

As it turned out, the third time they went, Dana got talking to the Tail Walker, the person at the back who makes sure everyone is safe, and told her how she didn't like college and what she liked on TV; her mother walked away to let them talk. That afternoon, Dana told her mother she really enjoyed the Park Run; her mother also felt good about it. Dana felt a part of something, and a little more connected to her local community.

Actions for Options

Options is about looking at your vision and asking, what can be done to move their relationship towards this goal? Some options for some stops will be immediately obvious now you've written the stop and objective down; for others, it may take some time for you to decide.

Look at your life plan and ask if there is anything that can be done now to protect them against possible negative repercussions or outcomes from relationships. Are there any additional opportunities that you can find to help develop their interpersonal skills? Are there any relationships that are damaging? It isn't just time online that needs consideration, sometimes it's also time with people who have a negative or detrimental effect that needs limiting. Consider what opportunities can be used to increase your child's confidence when interacting with others. It is likely that there are plenty around if you look broadly enough.

Create

Relationships evolve with time, and the types of relationship we want and need change as we move through our lives. When it comes to moving relationships forward, we might use social stories as a tool with which to build their skills. Relationships, whether they are dynamic or static, often follow basic scripts.

Sometimes just understanding the difference between responding and reacting to what people say can also make managing interactions with other people less of a challenge. We need to generate a plan that moves our young adults forward so they get the best from their relationships.

Life cycles

Time changes us, the roles we play as people and our relationships with others also adapt and shift over time. We all follow the same basic life cycle: we start as children, grow to become young adults, find our way in the world, and then gradually years make us older, and we pass into old age. In each of these stages, we grow and change as people. Our relationships also move through a similar cycle of change and evolution. As time passes, we take on many different roles in relation to other people. Think of the various roles you've taken on in your life: child, sibling, parent, friend, mentor, and many, many more. This affects the relationships we have with those around us; we develop new relationships, while others ebb away. These experiences have changed and shaped you. In short, these are the reasons why you are the person you are today.

When we have children, we take on the role of parent. First, our primary function is as nurturer and protector, and then we take on the role of teacher, as we demonstrate to our children how to live in and navigate through the world around them. After this, our next major function is to guide our children to adulthood, a process that is sometimes difficult with teenagers as they attempt to force their way into maturity. Ideally, we eventually reach an equilibrium as they live as adults. As we approach older age, perhaps we might turn to them for support and the parent/child relationship is reversed to some extent.

However, when we have a child with additional needs, this cycle is interrupted. The early stages may become significantly protracted, as the normal learning and growing processes are slower for our children. They may then need additional help to navigate the transition from teenage years to adulthood, and then, towards the end of our lives, they may never be able to take on the role of our guide, but instead need us to continue guiding and protecting them for as long as we are able. This is a real worry. We all know what happens at the end of our life cycle, and we need to make them as independent as possible before that day.

Social Stories™

Social stories can be used to explain in advance what comes next, and so help reduce anxiety. Carol Gray was a teacher for young students with autism in Michigan. In 1989, she began to write stories about common social situations and scenarios, to help share information that often seemed to be missing from their understanding of these situations and help guide how to behave in them – information we may take for granted, in particular the unwritten social rules that most of us understand implicitly. She noticed that reading these stories shortly before the event in question reduced their anxiety, improved the way they responded in these social settings, and enhanced their interactions. This idea became the Social Stories™: 'a social learning tool that supports the safe and meaningful exchange of information between parents, professionals, and people with autism of all ages' (www.carolgraysocialstories.com).

A social story is a personalised story written from the perspective of the individual with additional needs. It uses concrete examples and simple language to describe specific social situations and provides guidance on how to respond and behave appropriately. Social stories can be used to teach a wide range of social skills, such as greetings, sharing, taking turns, and managing emotions. They can also be an effective tool to help prepare your child for what lies ahead. We can use a social story to share information about how our relationship with our child may alter over time, and they can also be extended beyond your immediate relationship, to show how they will become more independent, perhaps interacting and getting support from others. You might explain who those people might be and how they can help.

The structure of a social story typically includes an introduction that sets the scene, a middle that describes the behaviour or situation, and a conclusion that provides a positive outcome or solution. The story may also include visual aids, such as images or photos, to help illustrate the narrative. Social stories are intended to be read and reviewed multiple times to help people understand and internalise social expectations and behaviours. The repetition and consistency of the story can help build confidence and reduce anxiety in social situations by providing a clear framework for understanding and responding to social cues.

As an example, the sort of social story I told my daughter when she was getting towards the end of school went something like this, but in language my daughter could understand, and in smaller snippets: 'Growing up can be scary and confusing, but it's also an exciting time. As you become an adult, you start to have more say in your life and the things you do. You start to think about what you want to do at college and after college finishes. You will need to think about what job you want to do, and what would be the best course to get you to it. You will also need to take on more responsibilities, like balancing your money, managing your calendar, and making your own appointments with people. These things might seem a lot at first, but there is technology to help. The thing to remember is everyone grows up and develops at their own pace, and it's OK to ask for help when you need it. All of us care about you and want you to succeed. As you become an adult, you'll start to figure out what makes you happy and what kind of person you want to be. You might have a few setbacks along the way, but you've always got over difficult things in the past. You have to take pride in who you are. You will do amazing things.'

Conversation scripts

Conversation scripts, with prewritten dialogues or prompts, are used to guide and structure conversations. These scripts can be in the form of visual aids and written instructions. They typically provide clear and concise information. The goal is to help your child learn social communication skills by providing a structured framework for social interactions.

While conversations with close people vary enormously, conversations with people we do not know well often follow a fairly basic structure. Learning how to converse with acquaintances and strangers can often be done with scripts. You can write your own scripts to suit your child and the social situations they encounter. Because these interactions tend to be relatively formulaic, some generic phrases can be learned. By gradually adding extra phrases at the beginning and end of these scripts, the conversations and interactions grow. The more scripts they have for specific occasions, the greater their confidence in having conversations with people.

Conversation scripts can be personalised to your child and their particular situations, scenarios, and contexts, and practised in a variety of settings to show your child how to start a conversation. It may also include prompts for different situations or topics, such as asking about the other person's hobbies or sharing information about their interests. Over time, with continued use and practice, they will learn to apply these same social communication skills more generally and in different contexts.

A visual example of a conversation script that uses picture symbols to prompt and structure a conversation might go something like this:

This script provides visual prompts and cues to help guide them through a conversation. It breaks down the different components of a conversation and provides clear instructions on what to say and when to say it. This helps to reduce anxiety, sets expectations, and allows them to feel more confident and secure during social interactions.

Responding versus reacting

At numerous points every day we either respond or react to events; this also happens with things said in relationships. We *respond* to things all the time, but we all know that not *reacting* is sometimes difficult. If you can explain the difference between the two to your child, then maybe they can learn why responding to something is always better than reacting to it.

Reacting to situations is not confined to people with additional needs: most of us are guilty of reacting to situations rather than responding to them at some point. Emotion takes over. Someone says or does something which causes us to behave in a way we would not consciously choose, but in the heat of the moment, it happens. With siblings, for example, one does something to the other and the fallout quickly seems like a war. Neither sibling pauses for a moment to consider what they are doing.

Knowing this happens is the first step to changing behaviour. An awareness of those things that annoy them may help your child learn to respond more and react less. Going back to the sibling example, you could try to explain their sibling's behaviour in a way they might understand. Perhaps you could link it to their sibling's age, and encourage them to be the adult by not reacting. Recognise, however, that as with all sibling relationships, there will always be emotion, competition and rivalry.

RYAN'S STORY

Ryan spends a great deal of time at home. Because he only goes out to a community centre half a day per week, he does not have many opportunities to develop his communication skills, but his parents have come up with a plan. The next time they take him to the doctor, they plan to improve his conversation skills with the aid of a rehearsed script.

They rehearse with him what he should say when he gets to the surgery. At home, when he isn't nervous, he gets it perfect each time. The next day, when he attends the surgery, he goes up to the receptionist and says, 'I'm here to see the doctor.' This was not quite as his parents hoped, because he didn't say his name and the receptionist had to ask for it. However, he did answer her questions.

At the next appointment, his parents coached him to say his name and the doctor's name.

This time he said to the receptionist, 'Hello, my name is Ryan. I'm here to see Doctor Moretti at 10.30.'

Spurred on by this little triumph, they transferred this script to another setting – his dentist's surgery. This time Ryan was able to repeat the script perfectly. Because of this, Ryan gained the feeling that he was able to do something for himself. His parents were happy and decided to start thinking about using other scripts in other contexts to keep building his confidence.

Actions for Create

Create is about deciding how you are going to teach them what's required for each stop, so how are you going to do this? Look through your list and decide what you are going to use for each stop on the Relationships line.

For some relationships, particularly static relationships, a script might be a good method. Scripts can also work as conversation starters for dynamic relationships, like asking what a friend has been doing or enquiring about the health of a relative.

For more complex relationships you might decide to use a social story to help them negotiate the more difficult parts, particularly navigating through different life cycles. Social stories might be a way of helping them to respond to difficult situations when they occur, rather than react to them. No doubt you will use various and multiple strategies all at the same time.

Assess

While relationships are always in a constant process of subconscious assessment because they modify and adapt as people grow and circumstances change, there are still times when your child's relationships with others should be more formally and consciously assessed. Major life changes like changing schools, entering college, or moving on from college to whatever is next will all introduce new types of relationships for which they might need preparation, new tools and enhanced skills. We also need to judge whether they have sufficient people in their life and the quality of their social interactions. Without contact with people, we get lonely and sometimes forget some of the conventions of communicating with others that have previously become quite familiar.

What has worked?

Relationships cannot be taught so they get a pass mark like an exam; however, they still need to be assessed. The key is giving your child strategies to help manage relationships more effectively. Scripts are the easiest way to begin to develop conversational skills, and are good for strangers and people they occasionally see. Often the interaction is confined to an exchange of information, and so one way to assess their progress is by how well they give and receive this information.

Did they get what they wanted from the person they spoke to? This can be seen illustrated in Ryan's story, where his parents assessed Ryan's success at the doctor's and then modified his script in preparation for the dentist.

Scripts can also be useful when meeting family they have not seen for a while. They could ask, 'How have you been?' Similar phrases that start conversations could be asked of friends too, so it is a transferrable script for several situations in which they have not seen someone for a while.

Perhaps a better indicator of progress is whether they respond or react when people say things they don't like. Do they lose their temper, or do they pause for a moment to consider their response? Do they take this as a cue to implement some of those breathing and calming strategies you have tried to instil in them to de-escalate situations? Obviously pausing and showing restraint is not something everyone can do all of the time, but if it is something they display occasionally, it shows progress.

Relationships are never easy, and empathy can be difficult to master. People act in illogical ways and fault does not always lie with our young adults, but the result of your child not being able to maintain relationships can be loneliness. One quality you could evaluate is their ability to be empathetic. While this is often regarded as something akin to emotional intelligence, it is actually a skill that can be taught. For example, when we make a mistake with a friend, we can either ignore it or reflect upon it. This process of stopping to take time to reflect can be taught. As part of the process, we could ask questions like, did I do anything to make that person behave in that way? If we conclude we were at fault, perhaps after reflection we might even feel an apology is warranted. Equally, the fault could also lie with the other person. This is also something we need to discuss. It is worth noting that if your child's empathy skills have improved, it may be because they are either maturing or learning new relationship skills. Both of these are good things and should be celebrated!

However, we should not get too preoccupied with empathy. Although having strong empathy skills is a good way of enhancing any relationship, we have all met people who do not have a great degree of empathy yet are highly regarded by society. Empathy is a scale; not everyone scores highly.

Finally, take a moment to evaluate their relationship with you. This is a good indicator of how well they understand relationships that change and evolve. If they engage with and adapt to this change, this suggests an increased understanding of how dynamic relationships develop and evolve over time. This can be a useful transferrable skill.

KIARA'S STORY

Kiara's parents know that Kiara is going through a rebellious phase. She's at that stage when young adults want to assert independence from their parents, but they are not always sure when or how to do so. As they look at her, they see a girl who is a great deal more pleasant to others than she is to them. With them she seems to argue simply for argument's sake and often over the smallest thing.

They realise the time has come when they need to tell her what to do less, and instead give her more space in which to grow and become her own person. They know that the power dynamic that exists between them as parents and her as a child must change, otherwise it is they who are holding her back emotionally, but they aren't quite sure how to do this.

They decide to talk to her with the aid of a social story. They cut out photos and put them on blank A3 sheets. The title is simple: *Becoming an Adult*. The introduction shows a girl roughly Kiara's age with the words 'Growing up and becoming an adult can be challenging, especially when it comes to arguments with parents.'

The main part of the story explained that 'When young adults start to take on more responsibilities and make more decisions for themselves, disagreements can arise. It's important to remember these arguments don't mean parents don't love you or don't want what's best for you. Sometimes they just have different ideas about what is best, and that's OK.

'When we argue, it's hard to stay calm and be nice. We should take deep breaths. We could use sentences beginning with "I" to express how we feel, like "I feel frustrated when I'm not given choices," instead of "You never let me do what I want." It's important we listen to each other's point of view. We might find we have more in common than we think. If a conversation starts to get heated, it's OK to take a break or walk away for a while. It's better to take a break than to say something hurtful we cannot take back.'

The story concluded: 'Communication, respect, and compromise are key components of any healthy relationship, including your relationship with us. With patience and understanding, we can work through arguments to find common ground. Remember growing up and becoming an independent adult is a journey, and it's OK to stumble along the way.'

They used simple pictures to show different emotions that might be experienced during an argument, such as frustration, anger, or sadness. They showed different ways to communicate feelings and opinions, such as speaking calmly and speech bubbles with sentences beginning with 'I feel ...' They always kept in mind it was vital to use images that were clear, easy to understand, and related to Kiara's individual experiences. They showed the importance of listening to the other person's perspective, with images of two people talking and listening to each other. They used screenshots of common situations in which arguments might occur. They included images of people hugging to show the argument was resolved.

After they finished discussing this with Kiara, they had a general talk about their own experiences when they were young and the relationship they had with their parents. They discussed what happened as they got older, and how their relationship with their parents changed. They also talked about Kiara's sister and described how, although they have a good relationship with her now, there was a time when it was difficult. When she was Kiara's age, she had found her parents boring and out of touch, with old-fashioned opinions and attitudes, but things were now a lot better.

They finished by saying to Kiara that her relationship with them is changing, and that's quite normal. They won't always agree about things. As her parents, they will always love and support Kiara whenever she needs it. Over time, and with repeated readings of the story, things began to improve.

Actions for Assess

Assess is a time for reflection and thinking of ways to improve relationships. It is not a place to despair at how complicated relationships are for all of us. The life plan is to remind you of your original vision for relationships and to determine how they can move closer to your vision and what you defined as successful relationship management.

Relationships are difficult to maintain but most people need other people, so regular appraisals of progress should be made in terms of the quality of the relationships in your child's life. Whether they respond or react to situations and if they are becoming more empathetic are both signs of progress and maturity in the way they manage their relationships. Take a moment to ask yourself, overall, is your child making progress?

Legacy

Legacy on the Relationships line can never be a single endpoint or skill. Relationships are always fuzzy around the edges, changing and evolving. If your child understands this and knows that people don't always act as logically or consistently as we would like, then they may cope better with people. If they understand something about the different life cycles people go through, then this knowledge will allow them to mentally prepare for when things change, which can reduce some of the stress for them.

In practice, this means knowing how to interact with people in the moment. Sometimes it's about having a bank of scripts in their heads that they use in different situations. The scripts might be just conversation starters to get them going or more complete conversation guides. One part of our legacy might be them knowing which starter to use for which conversation, and how to carry on that conversation once it has been started. This skill might be the key they need to form friendships and develop more rewarding relationships with family. Other times it's knowing that you can't change people to how you want them to be, and when a relationship or friendship doesn't work out, it is not necessarily anyone's fault; that's just the way it was meant to be.

What they will always remember, though, is your example to them. How they observe you treating people is how they will believe they should treat people. How you speak to them is how they will speak to you, and how you speak to others will be replicated in their communication. Sometimes we all get frustrated with the world, but it is a case of trying to remember how we would hope to be treated ourselves when others are frustrated by us.

We can also show them an important example of a dynamic relationship in transition: our relationship with them. We can give them a lesson on how these relationships should be navigated as people change and mature into a new cycle in their life. This is a valuable lesson on how to deal with relationships that need renegotiation from time to time. If they take this as a lesson on what sometimes happens in a relationship, it can be a transferable skill to other close relationships.

With our children and young adults with additional needs, it's sometimes easy to believe that they don't need relationships because they don't appear to want them. However, it's important to consider that maybe the real reason they seem reluctant is because they find them difficult and challenging. Giving them the skills to have relationships on their terms and when they choose is freeing them from loneliness. That is your legacy. Isolation happens when people cannot interact. That is why the Relationships line is so utterly vital in their life plan.

OUR STORY: Best friends

When my girls were young, we lived in a village. Our eldest became friendly with our neighbour's daughter of the same age before preschool, and they were inseparable for years. They are still close now, twenty years later.

Our youngest also formed a close friendship with a girl in her class. As we walked to school our daughter often shouted over the fence to her friend in the playground, 'I'll be there in a minute,' and quickly ran through the gates.

In summer, after school, it seemed like half the school played on the village green. My youngest, her friend, and a couple of others always rushed to the swings. I would chat with other parents while my daughter played with her friend, and however long she stayed it was never long enough. This girl made my daughter feel special in what was often a difficult and unfriendly school environment.

Everything changes eventually. We pulled our daughter out of that school when she turned ten. Our daughter didn't understand. She wanted her friend. She didn't want me home educating her, even if it was only temporarily. Even though she has developmental language disorder (DLD) and couldn't communicate her feelings, I knew she thought school-age children like her went to school, that's what they do. 'Why aren't I doing it?' she was probably asking herself.

My daughter's friend has since moved to another country. Perhaps this was just a stage in their lives, different life directions have led them down different paths, but we still look back with fondness, and our daughter continues to cherish this past friendship. Sometimes we regret what we have to do as parents, especially when it hurts our children, but my daughter was lucky enough to have that friendship at that time and it was a pleasure for us to see that she could build and maintain a close and meaningful relationship, even if it came to an end perhaps sooner than we would all have liked.

The Relationships line in context

The Relationships line is integral to all the other lines. When they live without us, they will live with or around other people. They will have to interact and make compromises with others in their household, or around where they live. They will need to be able to express their feelings and frustrations about the little things that others do that annoy them; they will also need to accept the same conversations back. Knowing this means we should discuss this with them and, as much as possible, prepare them to deal with this.

In a workplace or voluntary setting, they will have to maintain relationships with colleagues. They will need to understand that sometimes people say things they may not mean, and also that not everything should be taken literally. They need to have an idea of appropriate conversations in the workplace, and understand that when things are said that are unacceptable, improper or even offensive, there are steps that need to be taken and it can't simply be ignored. They will also need to know boundaries on the personal information they share with colleagues.

In life, most of us confide in someone in particular, usually a partner or very close friends. Occasionally we might choose to confide in a mentor. You may find you need more than one: there might be a mentor for more personal matters and another for financial. At times they might need to discuss a medical issue or need assistance getting the right healthcare. For this to happen, they need to trust someone enough to speak to them, and this may require a different person for each scenario. Mentors are a good idea; I certainly hope to find the right ones for my daughter.

Understanding the key importance of the Relationships line can help us to prioritise key skills and knowledge for a life plan to work. It can inform us about the areas of learning we should concentrate on and those things that can safely be ignored, and it will instigate a unified direction of travel.

Relationships constantly change and none of us can say we truly understand or have 'mastered' relationships. It is always a learning process. Perhaps one secret to successful relationships is developing empathy. When our young adults make a mistake or get relationships wrong, we may need to encourage them to reflect on what happened, why, and the impact it had on themselves and the other person. Conversely, we may need to reassure them that occasionally when a relationship breaks down, nothing they could have done would have prevented it – the relationship has simply run its course.

The Relationships line has the most profound effect on our young adult's mental health. How our children maintain relationships will improve as they grow in experience and maturity. We need to help them form a vision of what relationships should be like, pushing them to be as active in them as they can be but not pressing them beyond their limits. If we feel our life matters to other people, we feel valued. When we approach the end of our life, it is the relationships we've had that matter the most, more than any possessions or money. Having meaningful relationships in our life is essential to our mental wellbeing, and the same is true for our children.

FOUR

The Purpose Line

A significant part of most life plans is what people do with their day, because with a sense of purpose comes a sense of self-value. If our young adults don't have anything to do after full-time education ends, they may feel there is little point to their day. In this absence, there is a presence, and that presence is boredom. They may become less motivated for life and perhaps spend a great deal more time than you'd like looking at a screen, trying to fill time. It is worth noting that it may also make making and maintaining relationships harder: often what people do in their day is what they talk to other people about in conversations.

The Purpose line on the Red Giraffe Route Map is all about finding an activity for your child's day that has meaning so they feel they have contributed in some way. It's about how they add value to their community or other people's lives, but it is also about giving them a sense of their own worth. Purpose can be either a paid or a voluntary role.

Despite its fundamental importance, identifying a purpose is often a stumbling block for parents and children alike. As already mentioned, employment statistics for young adults with additional needs aren't good; in England adults known to their local authority in paid work is just 5.1%,[4] but a life plan can help your child beat these odds. Their overall happiness, mental wellbeing, and self-confidence may well depend on this part of their life plan being successfully and imaginatively completed.

Purpose often relies heavily on the Relationships line. Whether work, volunteering, or activity of whatever kind, it is inevitable that our young adults will have to deal with other people to a certain extent. This may require them to step up and behave more maturely; simply through the process of acting it, they will gradually become more mature. They will need to learn the unwritten rules about what should and should not be said to work colleagues, to the public, and to their friends. They learn much of this from the other stops along the Relationships line – it gives them a starting point from which to develop and scripts to use.

---

4   Mencap, www.mencap.org.uk/learning-disability-explained/ research-and-statistics/employment-research-and-statistics, accessed July 2023

From the Daily Living line, our young adults will bring skills to the workplace, but they will also learn new skills that they can apply to other areas of their lives.

It is hard to overstate the importance of purpose. Our purpose gives us our place in life, therefore as parents, we must absolutely, and at all costs, presume a purpose to their day if we are to make it happen. We start with our ideal vision and work through the stops until we get to either a paid or a voluntary role. We owe this to our children to ensure their lives have the purpose they deserve.

Vision

What purpose our children have varies from person to person, depending on their abilities, personality, interests, and their stage of life. Most people need a purpose to their day to reinforce their identity: we say we are a teacher, builder, or artist, or we can say we volunteer or work with a particular company, charity, or community group. If we do not have a purpose, we can struggle with this sense of identity, and this can adversely affect our confidence and mental health because purpose brings us into contact with other people and establishes connections and conversations.

What's possible is for us to believe there will always be something for our young adults to do. This should be discussed with them as much as possible because they need to see the journey ahead so that they will also presume a purpose. The key question you need to address is what will your young person do with their day when full-time education finishes?

At a bare minimum, the answer must be an activity that gives them a sense of being of value. What that might be depends on their ability and the opportunities available in your area, but we should not let our imagination or limiting beliefs hold us back from an optimistic and ambitious outlook. All too often, our own fears, anxieties, and lack of imagination are the true factors that limit our children, rather than any facet of the young adults themselves.

Stops on the Purpose line

It is likely that most stops on the Purpose line will be familiar. The only exceptions might be the final two stops: volunteering and paid work. Of course, paid work is not a suitable option for everyone, but volunteering is just as valuable. Both serve to give our young adults a purpose, a sense of value, and help contribute to their identity. Getting your child to this point is a great success and should be celebrated as such.

Some of our young adults will pass through every stop, others will skip stops, but they should still end up at the place you want them to be. We need to think about each stop carefully.

- **School** is the starting point for nearly everyone (and this includes home-schooling).

- **Work Experience** is a stop that is either found for them by their education provider during their school years, or we might find a placement for them.

- **Further Education** usually follows school and is similar in many ways.

- **Supported Internships** is more of a planned stop. This stop involves a job coach. It is usually unpaid while the training is being delivered, but with the expectation that paid employment will be offered at the end.

- **Volunteering** is a purpose and should be celebrated as such. It gives our young people a role to perform, from which a part of their identity can be formed.

- **Paid Work** not only provides a purpose but also an income.

Perhaps more than any other line, Purpose needs your active management. We need to ensure that our children travel through the stops, eventually reaching either of the last two stops on the line.

What would you call success?

Success should only have one definition: they have obtained a purpose to their day. The exact nature of that purpose, though, should not be defined too narrowly; it can be any activity in their day that makes them feel useful.

Along this line, however, the stops should have a more narrow definition of success.

- **School:** Success might be an enjoyable place to be where they engage in education and learning.

- **Work Experience:** Success might be anything that opens their horizons and builds their skills and confidence.

- **Further Education:** Success might be identifying and enrolling on a course that opens up the next opportunity for them.

- **Supported Internships:** Here success might simply be getting one! However, these opportunities are now more common than most people realise and should be welcomed for the other opportunities that often follow.

- **Volunteering:** Success for Volunteering (and other community roles and activities) should be defined as a feeling of achievement and of making a contribution.

- **Paid Work:** Success here is perhaps easier to define, often simply in terms of job titles and remuneration. However, there are other more subtle and less tangible manifestations of success, such as the feeling of achievement and validation that others value their work highly enough to pay for it.

The reason we need to aim for these successes is to take our young people in the right direction to a place that is filled with something to do after full-time education finishes.

DANA'S STORY

Dana's mother has wanted to keep Dana in college for as long as possible. She did not have a better plan or any idea of what else Dana could do, and so she was delighted each time the principal found Dana another course to enrol on, even when it was a sideways move to another level 1 course. She assumed Dana would never get a job because of her lack of maturity.

The problem is that Dana doesn't want to go to college anymore; her mother is terrified by this. She sees leaving full-time education as being like a cliff edge, where it will be too much screen time at the bottom of the fall. Dana doesn't cope without routine, and her mum fears nothing to do might also lead to isolation and depression as Dana's world shrinks around her.

Dana's mum doesn't know what to do. All she sees around her are other parents in the same position. All except one woman. She suddenly remembers the mother of a boy in the year above Dana. Although she and this woman never really spoke, she did hear that the young man had got himself a job for ten hours a week at a café. That had surprised her somewhat, but it also got Dana's mother thinking. If he could get a job, Dana should also be able to get a job, because she always thought their children's abilities were roughly the same.

She could also see that she had to change. If her limiting belief kept her thinking there weren't any jobs, she wouldn't see opportunities when they arose. She, as Dana's mother, needed to change what she believed. She first had to picture Dana working before she could convince Dana that she could be working; one follows on from the other. She realised she had work to do and began the process of challenging her limiting beliefs and visualising a better future for her daughter.

Actions for Vision

The presumption of purpose is a vital part of our vision. We must strive for either paid or voluntary work. More than anything else, this is a case of going through the stops and staying directionally correct until success arrives. For this reason, stops on the Purpose line are more of a linear plan than stops on the other lines. Your child will go through certain experiences, usually in turn, that lead them to whatever they eventually do after full-time education finishes. We must develop the right attitude and challenge any beliefs we may hold that are keeping our children back. Moreover, we must presume our child will end up having a worthwhile purpose to their day if we are to instil this belief in them.

Go to the bonuses at www.whatspossibleplan.com/ resources for a download to decide on your stops on the Purpose line. If you use the list of stops as a starting point, this exercise should not take very long.

Some stops, like work experience, may be revisited several times because no-one can have too much work experience and it can be incredibly useful for deciding the direction your child wishes to take. The overall direction your child must travel in is a presumption of purpose. Their life will be happier and more fulfilled if they have this, and it may do more to protect their mental health than most of us realise.

Options

More than other lines, our options are dictated by where we live. If you live in a city, there are probably more opportunities available simply because there are more people near you who can offer openings for our young adults. However, that is not to say that opportunities don't exist everywhere, and we must sometimes make our own luck. We should certainly look around to discover all our options, and as with Dana's mum, look for inspiration wherever it might be found.

The barriers

When considering the barriers to our children obtaining a purpose, it is easy to assume that it is our children's needs that prevent them from getting a worthwhile purpose. For some, it may be, but for many others, this may be incorrect, and it is important therefore that we take a moment to step back and challenge this assumption. We must be careful not to underestimate them, or automatically assume their needs are a barrier to purpose and use this as an excuse not to look for options.

There are more opportunities out there than many people realise. If you know one person with additional needs that has a job, then this is proof, first, that there are opportunities available, and second, that it is possible for someone with additional needs to take that opportunity. You should ask the organisation, person, or their family how it happened. Look to learn from their experience, even if the same opportunity is no longer available or would not be suitable for your child. This should motivate you to start your search for your child; do try to engage them in the process too.

Most organisations want to be an inclusive workplace and appreciate that this is part of their wider social responsibility. Some of their staff may already come from supported internships provided by global organisations like Project Search, national organisations, or other local providers. These organisations are a great place to start your search, and they usually have good contacts with local employers. It is a matter of locating these organisations, finding the best fit for your child, identifying the entry criteria and then planning three or five years ahead to make sure you are best placed to ensure your child meets these.

Another good place to search for ideas is the Expanding Worlds podcast. It constantly unearths possibilities all over the world, and not just in large cities. Although the organisations featured may not be in your area, they may offer ideas and possibilities that might lead you to something closer to home. The series *Ways Into Work*, starting at Episode 89, is a good place to begin.

The secret is to make sure it is not you holding back your child because of your unchallenged preconceptions and beliefs, and be relentless in your search.

Work experience

While the focus is to find purpose after full-time education finishes, we should not ignore the options available to them while they are still at school. For example, where possible you should support your child to get work experience, possibly a part-time job if available, or take on a volunteering role.

One of my regrets is not securing any of these for my daughter. It would have been a great opportunity for her to learn and I feel my daughter would have benefited from this. Two young adults in our friendship circle did have jobs while still at school – one in a charity shop, and the other in a supermarket – and I saw the positive impact it had on them both. My lack of imagination and belief in my daughter held her back.

Job carving

One idea to be aware of is job carving. Job carving is breaking down a job into different parts, and then giving just one part of that job to one person. On the Expanding Worlds podcast, Episode 85, *Pure Innovations: looking at what we can do differently*, the guest Neil Willows gives an example of how job carving works.

During the pandemic, hospital porters were given the extra task of sanitising the wheelchairs after use. This new job took extra time which meant porters had less time available to move the increasing number of patients. This is where job carving came in. The role of sanitising all the wheelchairs was given to a young person on a supported internship. While the benefit to the hospital was two-fold – the wheelchairs were thoroughly sanitised while giving porters back the time they needed to move patients – we can also assume that the young person gained an enhanced sense of value and purpose from doing this important task during an unprecedented global event.

Job carving can be hugely beneficial to employer and employee alike, in both the paid and voluntary sectors. Jobs can be carved up in a way best suited to particular employees who might prefer certain roles and tasks over others, but also in a way that best serves the employer. In short, job carving offers many possibilities and can open up additional roles in many organisations.

From the various examples we have explored, we can conclude that there can be a purpose for almost everyone, and that their additional needs should not be the thing restricting our search for a purpose for our child.

RYAN'S STORY

Ryan's parents never expected him to find a job. They assumed he would end up spending hours alone in his room. He doesn't go out to meet friends and his lack of activity is beginning to impact his health. He has frequent doctor's appointments but things don't seem to be improving.

His father's heart condition was a shock to them all and made his parents think. What will happen to Ryan when they aren't around? Where and how will he live?

As chance would have it, while waiting at the doctor's surgery, Ryan saw a poster on the notice board calling for volunteers. Something about supporting people who are homeless at the local community centre. He wanted to go even though his mum didn't think it was a good idea. She was worried about how he might feel when he got there and about what people might say to him, but he insisted because he wanted to do this for himself.

When he arrived, Ryan was asked to do the dishes. As the weeks passed, he started to really enjoy volunteering, and once, when another volunteer couldn't make it, Ryan stepped up to help serve the meals. He was nervous at first but, because he had got used to speaking for himself at his doctor's surgery, he was able to cope. The team leader was so impressed she asked him to stay in that role permanently. His mother was so proud when he told her.

Gradually he began to think of this as his purpose, and it made him feel valued. At his next doctor's appointment, he explained in detail what he did at the community centre. The doctor noticed an improvement in his health too.

His mum reflected; you don't know what you don't know. They would never have thought such a small change would have such a big impact on the way Ryan viewed himself and the confidence he now had. He believed in himself and his own value to the community. For Ryan and his parents, the value of this was priceless.

Actions for Options

Options is about looking at your vision and asking, what options are there to accomplish each Purpose stop on your child's route map? How can you help them get that first volunteering opportunity? Is there anyone you know who can help? Maybe a friend of a friend, or a neighbour of that work colleague of yours. Getting experience is important because the first thing employers often ask is, 'What experience do you have?'

Because the Purpose line is generally linear, we need to think ahead to what's coming up next in their lives and think about what options there are available. Before education finishes, find out if there is a good provider of supported internships near where you live, and if so, have you registered with them? We need to be aware of what's next and begin to pave the way for the following stops, sometimes a year or more ahead.

However, the single most important thing we must do is not to underestimate our young adults. We must presume they will get a purpose to their day; it should be at the front and centre of everyone's life plan for their child, and we must instil this belief in our children too. We must ask, 'What's possible?' If barriers lie in the way, how can we overcome them? What steps can be taken now to make the way easier in the future? We must look for options and contact organisations that offer these types of opportunities. We should help them find any job available and encourage them to volunteer.

Create

When it relates to purpose, Create tends to mean planning the stops along the line. Teaching is often done by you, but also by others, possibly through school or an organisation. There are things we can do to make the process of moving along the line and transition easier for all concerned. You can give your child a presumption of purpose.

Working, whether paid or voluntary, is made up of two elements. The first component is doing what's required, performing the tasks so they get done. Some tasks are easy; others require a little more skill and training. The second is attitude. This is less about the skills involved in the job and more about our willingness to work. A good attitude is something a lot of employers value over ability. The good news is you can teach your child to have a positive attitude, which will give them an advantage over many others.

Create a presumption of purpose

It's easier to achieve something if we already presume it is possible. To *presume a purpose* is to suppose it will happen one day, an informed guess based on reasonable evidence; conversely, to assume a purpose expects it to happen but accepts that this might not be the case. The difference might be subtle, but it's an important mind-set change.

While they are still at school, you may explain the stops along the route, and as you show them these stops, it is also a good chance to explain the importance of them. A social story might be one way of showing the route your child will take as they move out of full-time education to the next part of their life.

As with most plans, the earlier we plan, the better. The end vision should be something discussed with them, so they can have input into where they hope to be in the years ahead. They will need to be part of the process as soon as they are able, even if you have started making plans long before they were ready to take part in the conversation.

You need to talk about this future often so they start to believe it will happen. You need to frame the words so they can repeat the story to others when asked about what they are going to do after they leave school; people, such as relatives and friends, will inevitably ask. It is by them buying into the story that they will come to believe in the presumption of purpose.

Attitude towards purpose

As mentioned above, a role, whether paid or voluntary, has two aspects: having the skills to do the job and having a good attitude. While some roles may require more skills than your young adult possesses, many organisations value attitude over specific job skills. Job skills can be learned, but a positive attitude is harder to teach.

In *Developing the Qualities of Success*, Zig Ziglar drew up a long list of qualities that employers look for in a potential employee. Among these are reliability, politeness, being on time, being willing to learn, being flexible, being prepared; the list goes on. He asks if you were an employer, would you reject someone with all these qualities? He believes the answer is no.

All of these qualities can be collectively thought of as having a good attitude because they bear no relation to one's ability to perform a task. You can discuss with your young adult why it's important to have these qualities. You can also discuss why an employer would value these qualities.

Developing this positive attitude can take time. Once my daughter and I were running late getting to her placement due to traffic. We spoke about the need to apologise. She replied, 'I don't need to. No-one else does when they're late, and they're always late.' I steered the conversation to how it seemed rude not to apologise for being late. At first, she did not agree because of the example set by others, but as we spoke about it more over the following days, she began to think it was important.

This is a social story I used with my daughter to reinforce how important attitude is at work. Using a social story like this can help your child understand expectations about their behaviour in the workplace.

I arrive 10 minutes before my start time.

I always look neat and tidy.

I follow my manager's directions.

I don't get distracted by or use my phone at work.

I am always friendly and polite to customers.

At the end of work, I leave everything tidy.

Work Attitude Story

My daughter's positive attitude to work sets her apart from many people she knows, and it will for your child too.

KIARA'S STORY

Kiara's parents had a vision of paid employment for her, but they also realised she didn't yet have the necessary skills to make her employable. They did as much as they could think of to move her forward, including finding her work experience at a charity shop, and before the end of college, they contacted an organisation that offered a supported internship. Kiara's parents helped her fill in the application form, and she had an interview with the provider organisation.

A week later, Kiara was offered a spot in the supported internship programme. She was assigned a job coach and offered a placement at a hotel. Her first few days were spent clearing and cleaning tables after guests finished breakfast. She was shown how to set a table and told the placement of cutlery and glasses needed to be exact; Kiara took a photo to remind her how to do it every time.

In the following weeks, assisted by her job coach, Kiara was asked to greet guests arriving for breakfast. She had to ask for their room number and check them off on a list. After she became familiar with that part of the script, other parts were added, including 'Please take a seat anywhere' and 'Please ask if you need assistance.' Her job coach gradually pulled away as Kiara became more confident. The manager was particularly impressed when Kiara one morning spontaneously said to a guest that was leaving, 'Have a nice day.'

At the end of the placement, Kiara was offered fifteen hours of paid work a week. Her parents had discussed what success would look like with Kiara, and this was it. Her parents took her out to her favourite restaurant to celebrate.

Actions for Create

Create is usually about what *you* can do to help move your child forward. On the Purpose line, however, Create will usually be done by others – schools, colleges, employers, and organisations for which they volunteer – but that doesn't mean you don't have anything to teach them.

To work, even on a voluntary basis, they need the right attitude. There are expectations surrounding what we do in a work environment, how we behave, and the things we don't do. All of these need teaching and this is where you come in. No employer or organisation ever says, 'We don't want people with a good attitude.' It can give your child an advantage over others and a competitive edge; this is a secret most people don't know. Think about how you can make your child of use and enthusiastic the moment they arrive. Making coffee or clearing up is a small skill taken from the Daily Living line, but it makes them an asset to have around.

The Purpose line also crosses over the Relationships line in how your child interacts with colleagues. They need to have certain scripts in their heads to help them navigate their conversation with colleagues and possibly customers.

Having a fully developed life plan will assist them to get the things in life they deserve. Sitting at home watching a screen, although they may desire it, is not what they really want or need. They want to feel valued and have a sense of self-respect, and this is often reinforced by having a purpose to their day.

Your child should have a presumption of purpose. They must see their future ahead of them after they finish education. As part of this, they need to develop a positive attitude towards having a purpose. With this positive attitude totally ingrained into who they are, the chances of them finding a worthwhile purpose are hugely enhanced.

You need to be constantly aware of and preparing for the next stage in their journey, the next stop. There are various practical steps you can do to make the path ahead smoother and easier to visualise, and it is important to prepare your child for their future, both psychologically and in a skill sense where possible.

Assess

When it relates to purpose, Assess is less about progress and more about the effectiveness of your plan to get them where they need to be next. At school, you assess progress with learning, but when it comes to college, we need to consider whether the curriculum being taught takes them closer to where they want to go and whether they have a presumption of purpose for themselves.

Assess where they are on their journey

They must presume their days after full-time education will have a useful activity and purpose. If they do not presume this, maybe you need to talk about their journey more. Think of examples and stories that will inspire them. Again and again, go over the next stops on their journey, and outline how one thing can lead to another. Explain that it may take time, but with persistence, it *will* happen one way or another.

You should take time to appraise their progress along the Purpose line. Is their current placement suitable? Will it lead to the next planned stop? Is what they are learning valuable or simply passing time? It is important to remember that not only should we plan their journey, we should also manage it to ensure each step really does lead towards the next stop.

If they do not get to the next stop you planned, what can you do to get them back on track? Are there other options? Sometimes even the most well-thought-out plans don't always go smoothly. Opportunities may not be as available at certain times, but commitment overcomes statistics, eventually. The challenge for you is to keep going; something will come along if you and your child persist.

Assess attitude

Finding a purpose for your child after full-time education takes a great deal of effort and so it's particularly important to ensure they have the right attitude for when one is found. Getting accepted for a role is one thing, keeping it if they have a poor attitude towards their work, their colleagues, timekeeping, and so on, is quite another thing. While your child's attitude is not under your control, it is under your influence and you must get this right with them.

While assessing attitude can sometimes be hard to gauge, especially when you are not with them all the time, indicators can be found in their attitude to you and others close to them. When they are asked to do something at home, do they do it without complaining? Is it done in a timely manner? Similarly, are they helpful to people? Not just you but other people. Are they willing to lend a hand? Do they ever take the initiative to help others? If they don't, this could simply be a lack of thought, but if they do, this is a good indicator of a positive attitude. Expectations might need to be outlined clearly because sometimes it is the little things that matter most in a work environment.

If there appears little or no progress, how can you change your message to improve their attitude? Do you need to set a better example? Does your family say one thing and do something else? This is not meant to be a dig at you, but there is no doubt that your child will follow the example you set.

MARSHALL'S STORY

Marshall got onto a supported internship. He got along well with his job coach and enjoyed the work in a small café. He preferred food preparation and the less customer-facing roles, but occasionally he was placed front of house, a position he disliked as he sometimes struggled to cope with customers. When this happened, his job coach would pull him aside and try to help him calm down.

The crunch came one Friday when his mother received a call. Marshall had become terribly upset, saying he didn't like customers and had refused to serve them. When he got home, he told his mother he wasn't going back.

Over the weekend both his mother and father spoke to him. They tried to explain that serving customers and selling coffee and cakes kept the café in business. As nicely as they could, they told him he had to learn to cope with customers.

Unfortunately, the decision was taken out of his hands. Over the weekend the café owner had also been doing some thinking. This wasn't a good match. While she wanted to give a young person with additional needs a chance, her café was too small for a choice of roles. She had to let Marshall go.

While they were disappointed, Marshall's parents tried to ensure he took something from what had happened. They told him he needed to think about what lessons he could take from this experience, and asked how he could use what he'd learned in the future. They said he had to go back to the classroom of the internship provider organisation to finish the academic year. They wouldn't let him quit.

He spent three weeks back in class. Behind the scenes, the provider organisation had been looking for alternative options for Marshall and was able to offer him a placement in the kitchen of a restaurant. He wouldn't have to face customers there, but he would still have to learn to work with his colleagues.

Marshall's parents breathed a sigh of relief. They were glad they hadn't given up, and Marshall was firmly back on his Purpose journey.

Actions for Assess

Unlike the other lines, assessment on the Purpose line is a continual process of assessing both the now and the future. It shouldn't only be done while they are at a particular stop, but you should also be continually looking to the stops ahead to make sure what is required hasn't changed, and that their current learning and development is leading them in the right direction. You will also need to evaluate how they are doing with their current activity and attitude. Are they mature enough for the next stage, and if not, what can you do to encourage the maturity needed? A life plan should be monitored, and this is especially true for Purpose. Too many of our young adults are needlessly stuck at home because of the lack of a plan.

As I have said before, it is important to remember that we should celebrate their successes with them. Let them know we're cheering for them and make it a special event when a milestone is achieved.

When you review progress, it should be fairly evident whether your child is working with the expectation that they will one day have a purpose to their day. As part of this, ask yourself whether they also have a positive attitude towards work. It's important they develop both the skills and the right attitude that they need to move forward. Sometimes we may need to adjust our plans or make alternative arrangements, but as long as we continue to head in the direction of voluntary or paid roles, they will find something that suits them. The hardest part for you might be staying on course and believing in the journey.

Legacy

Your legacy on the Purpose line is ensuring that they have activity in their day after full-time education finishes. Whether that activity is paid or unpaid shouldn't be the main concern. The primary goal of this activity is to ensure that they will get a place to go for part of their week, a change of scene and variation of routine, and possibly also some monetary reward. Above all, what this purpose really offers them is engagement with the world and their community, and a sense of value and worth.

Whatever the activity, this is experience that they can put on their résumé. When next they go for an interview, they can list what they have done. A mistake many parents fall into is believing that their child's first activity will be their job for life; everyone goes through numerous roles in their lives, and so will your child.

Maybe they won't remember their attitude and beliefs about work came from you, but they will remember the journey they have undertaken with you as they rightfully claim credit for the result. We can live with that. I'm so proud that my daughter is in paid work, and she rightly believes she has this because she focused on her goals. Debra and I had a plan, and every time a half-chance presented itself, we used the opportunity to reinforce a positive attitude about how people need a good work ethic to get and keep a job. These, now, are her beliefs, and she is truly valued in her workplace.

Again, let me emphasise: the goal isn't achieving paid work because not everyone will have the opportunity for this; a voluntary or community role gives the same sense of value that we want our children to experience and *this* is our goal. The point is for you to have no regrets at the end of your life about what you should've, would've and could've done. Regardless of what they do, imagine how proud you would be if they can say in conversation, 'I'm a ...' or 'I do ...' What they are really saying is, my role in life is *this*.

It is something to build their self-esteem around and comes directly from the attitudes you instilled in them. That is a legacy worth leaving.

OUR STORY: Towards employment

The natural progression for our daughter after high school was college. I hoped this would be a place where she would flourish and mature; maybe I was a little optimistic in my expectations. The focus of her college seemed to be on therapies – occupation, and speech and language – with less emphasis on employability skills and what would happen after college came to an end. Maybe that's the way the education system is designed, and perhaps there are funding restrictions I'm not aware of. While these therapies were great for my daughter's personal development, I couldn't picture how they would help her move to the next stop towards employment.

Quite some time before, on the Expanding Worlds podcast, Debra interviewed an organisation called Team Domenica, which offered a 'supported into employment' programme. From then on, this programme was in our plans for our daughter, but as we struggled with the limitations of the college system, we started to consider whether we should bring this stop forward. Just before the pandemic, Team Domenica advertised an open evening, and our daughter went along and liked the programme and the people.

Then, not long after, lockdown was imposed. Teaching at college became hastily assembled Zoom and Teams meetings; going out became walks in the woods with our dog, and an online fitness instructor called Joe Wicks became her morning routine. In lockdown, suddenly everyone got a taste of how our children with additional needs often feel – isolated, alone, and not easily able to communicate with family members and friends. If I ever doubted what my daughter's life would be like without a purpose, lockdown demonstrated that future to me.

When we had withdrawn her from mainstream school eight years earlier, I took on the role of home educator; this time Debra took on the main teaching role. She has teaching qualifications and was previously a teacher and lecturer at university, but like every other parent, she found lockdown classes difficult. If college wasn't working for our daughter *before* lockdown, it certainly wasn't any more successful *during*.

Our daughter had an online interview for Team Domenica. She was offered a place. We then faced an awkward decision: stay with a college that offered great speech and language and occupational therapy, or risk it for the unknown.

We agonised.

Then we remembered that sometimes, if you risk nothing by trying to stay safe, you can lose everything by not taking those opportunities that could lead to something so much better. It is sometimes a case of aiming higher into the unknown beyond rather than accepting something that has identifiable limits.

We discussed the offer with our daughter honestly. We explained it would mean a new setting, new people – everything would be different. Although this made her uneasy, she liked the idea of practical work more than a classroom, so she decided to accept and started at Team Domenica after the first lockdown ended.

Being on this programme was completely different to the college environment she'd been used to. Mandatory Maths and English lessons still followed her, but the focus was on more practical skills. To my surprise, she fully embraced serving customers at their training café. She liked front of house roles more than other jobs.

As she spent more time on the programme, she began to think of herself as an adult and, as she thought this, it became a self-fulfilling prophecy in that she matured faster than before. She took her responsibilities seriously and developed a positive attitude towards work and doing her job well.

Her programme was extended by a year because of the pandemic, and in her third year, she was offered a supported internship at an international hotel chain. As part of the support offered, she had a job coach who she got on with very well. Gradually she was given more and more responsibility, and her job coach always seemed to know the right moment to step back and leave her to do tasks on her own. She loved the hotel and her work there, and she felt part of a team; at the end of the placement, she was offered paid employment. Taking the risk into the great unknown was the best decision she could have made.

The Purpose line in context

With the Purpose line perhaps more than the other lines, the results of your teaching will become clear at a relatively early stage. In the UK, you know what they will be doing after full-time education by their early to mid-twenties; in the US, by twenty-one. Maybe this age difference is why there are many forward-thinking people in the US trying to address the challenge of life after full-time education early, sometimes in a holistic way by incorporating community, purpose, and a place to live. Many of the US organisations featured on the Expanding Worlds podcast demonstrate this.

What's needed is for all our young adults to have a presumption that they will always have a purpose, a job, or a voluntary role to occupy their day and give them a sense that they add value to society or their community in some way. To get our children to this stage, the Purpose line relies heavily on the other lines.

The more skills they can do on the Daily Living line the better. Our young adults can be useful the moment they enter the door of an organisation if they can use their initiative as much as possible when they notice something needs doing. Indeed, you should look to prioritise skills at home that are transferrable to a workplace setting.

A workplace will have colleagues and, possibly, customers. Strategies from the Relationships line may make the difference between them keeping a placement or losing it. Knowing how to act appropriately will need instruction, along with good personal habits and routines. Sometimes it's the little things like attitude that make the biggest difference to others, and it can be such a simple thing to get right.

The Purpose line is vital because everything else seems to run off it. Purpose, if paid, can contribute to income. Purpose encourages our children to engage with the world: it usually gives them people to interact with and can help prevent social isolation. A person with a purpose will have an identity, a sense of self-worth, and greater self-esteem. They will feel part of their community. This person can be your young adult.

FIVE

The Financial Line

E very life plan includes a section on finances, even if money and wealth aren't your main focus. Everyone needs money for their long-term security, but our young adults may rely more heavily on others to help plan and manage this security. For this reason, careful planning of the Financial line is imperative.

The previous three lines each enabled them to live a better life and become more independent. Daily living skills allow them to build their self-respect as they look after themselves in a physical sense and control their living environment. Better relationships allow them to connect with other people and their community, increasing their self-worth. Having a purpose to their day not only gives them a place to go but can also provide them with a feeling of value and a sense of identity. However, the thing that underpins their long-term future is financial security.

Warning: Everything that follows is for educational purposes only. It is not intended to be financial advice and should not be used as such. You should seek professional advice from someone suitably qualified, who can become familiar with you, your family, your family's finances, and your young adult's hopes and dreams for their future. Advice must be tailored specifically to your circumstances.

Vision

The central concern of the Financial line is how your child's finances will be organised. It all starts with deciding who controls their finances. Everyone wants to leave their children financially secure but the question is, how? At one end of the continuum is a guardianship, where their finances are fully controlled by someone else. At the other end is complete autonomy where they control all their own finances. In between are numerous other permutations. Each has advantages and disadvantages. We must decide the best way to offer our child financial security when we are not around to support them. For this, we need a vision of how their financial affairs will be organised.

Guardianships give complete control of their finances to someone else. The advantages of guardianships are beyond the scope of this book. There are many, and for some, this is the best option, not only to protect your child financially, but also to look out for their best interests, both physically and emotionally.

The premise of this book is to make our young adults as independent as possible; this might therefore suggest they should have as much control as possible over their own money. It is easy to accept that their money should be their money, but we may worry that they don't always appreciate the value of money, nor understand that it is finite. Our biggest fear is that they will run out of money and perhaps find themselves struggling with the cost of daily living, or even homeless. Many of us may worry about whether our children will be too trusting and at risk of being cheated out of their money.

We need to decide where and how their finances will be managed, on the continuum from no control to total autonomy. In all cases, our goal is to give them as much independence as possible, while also protecting them financially so they can afford the life they desire.

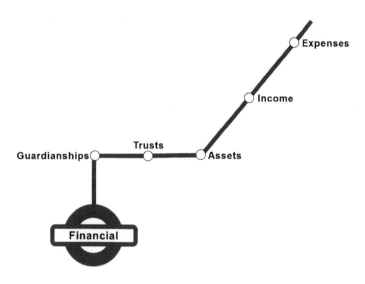

Stops on the Financial line

There are only a few stops on the Financial line:

- **Guardianships** enable you to bypass most of the other stops because your child will not need to learn how to manage their finances themselves; control of their money lies with their guardian.

- **Trusts** hold assets and money for beneficiaries, but our children do not have control over them.

- **Assets** are things your child may own themselves if you do not have a trust in place for them.

- **Income** usually comes through having paid work or through some form of government benefits.

- **Expenses** are those things they will need to pay for to maintain their lifestyle.

Our children will only have financial security if their expenses are always less than their income.

What would you call success?

Success should only have one definition: they have enough money coming in so they can live their life the way they want to. What this means will differ depending on our children's individual expectation.

Looking at the short term (perhaps the next three years), if they are living at home and in full-time education, success might be achieving one or more of the following:

- **Guardianships:** to arrange one; manage it effectively; and ultimately to have a plan to pass control to someone else.

- **Trusts:** to set one up; have a plan about who will run it and how it will be run in the future. If you plan on using a trust, it is very likely you will want to leave your assets to the trust rather than to your child to control.

- **Assets:** to make a will so the assets you currently own may be left to your child or their trust.

- **Expenses:** to set up one or more bank accounts and have them learn how to track how much they spend.

When they have left full-time education, medium-term success in five years might be:

- **Income:** to receive enough money to cover all monthly expenses from either working or government benefits, or a combination of both. This would include a working knowledge of how to manage their bank accounts and balance expenses. It may also include automated payments for bills and emergency savings.

These short- and medium-term aims are entirely hypothetical. If and how they relate to you and your child is a matter of judgement. The only non-negotiable is that you identify your definition of success.

MARSHALL'S STORY

Marshall doesn't have any money sense and the word 'restraint' isn't in his vocabulary. If he sees something, he wants it then and there. His mother has tried to teach him to check his money on the banking app, but because money is such an abstract concept to him, he hasn't grasped the fact that it runs out very quickly. He is sometimes naïve about the world, and they worry he could be too easily convinced to give away his money.

A larger issue in Marshall's story is that his parents do not agree over money. There is an ongoing issue over the financial support offered by his father and his father's second wife. She is unhappy about contributing to Marshall's welfare as she feels that they don't have enough for their own immediate family's needs, let alone to support Marshall too. Marshall's mother doesn't quite see it that way, especially when she sees their new car, but she needs to park these thoughts.

They need to come up with some sort of vision about how Marshall's finances will be organised. The last thing she wants is for him to be left unsupported should anything happen to her, and if anything happened to his father, she has no doubt that his father's other children would get priority over his inheritance. However, she also understands that they don't want to leave money for Marshall in her sole control, even if she would always use it solely for his benefit.

As much as she doesn't like the idea, she decides to investigate using a trust. She's always been reluctant before as they seemed so complicated but she quickly finds out that, with the right guidance, one could be established relatively simply. She speaks to Marshall's father. 'A reasonable compromise,' he agrees. They decide to set one up and speak to their lawyers about their wills.

Marshall's mother feels relieved that Marshall will have money set aside safely for the future, but there will also always be trustees around to protect him against people taking advantage of him. Marshall's father and his second wife are now arguing less as Marshall's finances are at last organised and agreed between all parties.

Actions for Vision

If your child is to live the life they want (and you want them to have), they must have financial security. Ideally they should have as much financial autonomy as possible because this encourages greater independence, but if you are leaving them money through inheritance, you have a right to expect it will be used wisely. Our children are disproportionately poorer compared to other groups in society; 27% of people with disabilities live in poverty compared to the average of 21%[5] so ensuring a sound financial future is imperative. Regardless of the exact solution or combination of financial options you elect to use, we need to organise their financial affairs to give them as much security as possible for when we are not around to support them.

Vision on the Financial line requires us to answer a key question: does my child need a guardianship to protect them? Often this is a matter of personal choice, but we should always allow them as much autonomy as possible. Not being financially literate is not, I believe, a reason to stop them from having control over their finances – many people aren't that financially literate, and yet they manage to get by. However, that's not to say you shouldn't use the tools available to protect major assets or inheritances they might receive.

Download the bonuses at www.whatspossibleplan. com/resources to decide on your stops on the Financial line. If you use the list of stops as a starting point, this exercise should not take very long. On the

---

5   The Health Foundation, 'Inequalities in poverty' (21 December 2022), www.health.org.uk/evidence-hub/money-and-resources/poverty/ inequalities-in-who-is-in-poverty, accessed July 2023

download, you might also want to include stops you need to make, such as making a will, setting up lasting powers of attorney, and death tax planning, to ensure your assets are used in the way you wish.

The Financial line is one of the scariest for everyone to think about, but think about it we must. Everything in our children's life plan is underpinned by the strategy for this line. It is important to define success for each stop on this line for your child's life plan, even if the final answer comes years later. Remember, *directionally correct* are the watchwords here.

Options

There are three broad options available. At one end of the continuum is Guardianships, in which complete financial control is handed over to an appointed guardian. The details of guardianships are beyond the scope of this book, but they certainly have their place and are certainly necessary to ensure financial security for some young adults.

Next to guardianships on the Financial line and close in terms of control are Trusts. You may intend to use something like a trust to hold assets, which means finding a balance between the finances your child controls and those controlled by the trustees. It is worth noting that if you use professional people as trustees, this will come at a cost to the trust.

At the other end of the continuum is the option of letting your child have complete control over their finances. This can be a worrying prospect for any parent but do remember that our children are frequently more capable than we imagine, and safety nets and plans can be put in place to help. Fixed expenses can often be managed by your child when you establish a workable system to control them, and many young adults are capable of working within clearly defined rules, if the purpose and rationale are explained to them in advance.

The stops on the Financial line that need the greatest evaluation are Income and Assets, and a consideration of whether to leave any assets, such as a property, in a trust. Whatever you do and however you decide to set up their financial affairs, they will need enough income to sustain the right lifestyle for them.

Income

When you are not around to support them, income will either come from paid work, government benefits, or assets you leave through inheritance. It could well be a combination of all these.

If your young adult gets paid work, there may be a question as to whether that income would be enough to pay for their lifestyle. A job might mean only thirty hours per week or fewer, which would leave them struggling to pay all their expenses, although government benefits might make up some of the difference.

Do remember that the purpose of a job is not purely financial, however, as covered in the previous chapter.

For some individuals, government benefits may be their main source of income. Depending on where you live and the needs of your child, the level of support will vary. In addition to this, as successive governments try to reduce expenditure, rules and benefits will continue to change. This may mean that your child will need someone to help them keep pace with regulatory changes in the future, and to ensure they continue to receive all they are entitled to.

Money from an inheritance, intended to contribute towards your child's living expenses, can cause a problem when applying for government benefits. Most benefits are means-tested; that is, if you have more than a certain amount of money in the bank, you do not qualify for assistance. Sometimes it is a case that they will not receive assistance before this money is spent. To mitigate this, many people put assets in trust for their children.

Income from a trust

Assets put in a trust do not belong to your child. This has important implications when applying for government benefits as the asset is not considered theirs and it cannot be regarded as money they have available. This is important if applying for means-tested benefits or other forms of financially assessed support, where having too much money available can prevent a successful application for government benefits. This is often the main reason why parents set up trusts for their children.

There are also other benefits to a trust. It can offer a degree of protection to your child as well as financial security. For example, if you leave the house in which they live to a trust, they will always have a place to live, but that house is not considered 'theirs'. This means that even if they are not good at managing their own money, they cannot get into debt to the point where their home is repossessed; similarly, they can't be defrauded out of it. Likewise, if they became romantically involved and the relationship ends, a partner could not claim half the asset because your child does not own it.

Setting up a trust is not as difficult as people imagine. Trusts for the most part follow the same basic pattern. There is a 'settlor' (the person who starts the trust), a 'beneficiary' (the person who gets money and assets from the trust), and a number of 'trustees' (people who run and administer the trust, and the legal owners of the assets held in the trust). Most trusts have at least two people as trustees, most likely starting with you. They can be set up by a lawyer or financial adviser, who will talk you through the process in more detail.

From my experience, setting up a trust is a great deal easier to do than deciding who future trustees might be. You could use professional people as future trustees, but this will come at a cost. Lawyers and accountants charge for their time, and over the years these costs can mount up. However, this option will ensure that the trust is likely to be well-managed and meet its legal and regulatory obligations.

If you choose a nonprofessional, there are certain things you should consider:

- Is this possible trustee young enough to be around for your child well into the future?

- Are they a good money manager themself?

- Are they willing and capable of handling the responsibility?

- Are they a good administrator? Being good with money is not the same as doing the necessary paperwork each year after the trust becomes active.

I would advise against any automatic assumption in favour of choosing family members as trustees. They may not be impartial and may not always follow your instructions as closely as paid professionals or slightly more distanced non-professionals might.

The life plan you have been working on throughout this book has been drafted for two sets of people: the primary focus is your child, to enable them to move towards greater independence; the second is for any-one supporting your young person. Initially, this is likely to be you as parents, but it is also for anyone who shares this role, now or in the future. You are producing a statement of wishes, to guide them on your aspirations, hopes, and dreams for your child. Whoever is in control of their finances needs to know your intentions so they can facilitate the financing of it.

Passing over greater control

At some point, you will want your child to take on a greater degree of control over their finances. While this is a huge milestone in the maturity of your child, this handover also signifies more than this: it is the start of you separating your finances from theirs.

When they are a child, their finances could be visually represented like this:

You have control over their financial affairs. You control income and manage all expenses like housing, utility bills, clothing, food, and leisure. They have a small amount of control within this, possibly with only their pocket money to spend.

As they get older, they may take on a greater degree of financial control. This might look something like this:

Here they have taken over most aspects of their finances, from paying for housing to utility costs, from clothing to leisure spending, and all else in between. They are by far the biggest financial player, but you may still have control, perhaps via a trust and the assets you have put in the trust. Your protective ring encloses their circle of control, however large it might be.

The size of the circle in the middle may vary from person to person. For example, a trust might pay their utility bills and housing costs, while they control all other aspects of their spending. The logic behind this could be to ensure they always have a home with the heating and lights on. The inner circle may be significantly smaller if their ability to manage their finances is more restricted, but it should always be as large as can be safely managed. When you are considering options, you want to ask how large that inner circle can safely be made. How much financial independence should we give them while, at the same time, maintaining their financial security?

KIARA'S STORY

On the Purpose line, Kiara's parents had defined success as fifteen hours of paid employment per week. Until she matures further, they don't know if she will be able to work more hours than this, but they hope it will come with time. Remuneration from these hours is not sufficient to support her lifestyle, let alone pay accommodation and utility costs. Her parents investigate government benefits and realise she could be eligible for top-up payments but only if they don't leave her their family home, which they had planned to do.

To get around this, they decide to set up a trust. As an accountant, her father knows that anything held in a trust is not classed as a personal asset. This means that when Kiara's application for government benefits is submitted, the value of the house would not be counted in means testing. They spend some time weighing up the options, trying to decide between setting up the trust now or to come into effect upon their deaths. Her father is a details man and prefers to set it up now so all the running details can be worked out well in advance. This enables them to make regular gift allowance contributions to the trust, and Kiara's grandparents also decide to leave their assets to the trust in their wills.

Kiara's parents' vision is for her to manage her day-to-day finances herself as far as possible. The trust may provide accommodation to her as the beneficiary and will also pay her utility costs and all other household bills. However, they still need to set up a system for Kiara to organise her personal finances and manage her spending.

Actions for Options

Income is of paramount importance to our children's financial security. Having sufficient income means having enough money to live on but does not necessarily mean enough to have everything they could possibly desire. We need to secure this income, while also creating a system to ensure that expenses are not allowed to exceed income. We must also choose whether to leave assets directly to them or in a trust. It is important to choose our options wisely because we want to protect their financial future so they can live the life they want while, at the same time, allowing them as much control over their finances as possible.

On your child's life plan, you should by now have determined the stops and provided some broad definitions of success. When considering how to move forward, the next step is to consider the options on the Financial line. Who will be their mentors or financial advisers? Who will be the trustees if a trust is involved? Who are those people who will help them when they cannot get the utility companies to fix a bill? What are the best options for organising the finances which they control? One bank account with different pots of money for different purposes, or several bank accounts? How will you find a lawyer to set up the legal framework? How will you find an accountant to give prudent advice to you on the best way forward to achieve the aims and objectives of their life plan? This is where having a life plan with all other areas of their lives mapped out in basic form helps because professional advisers can better understand your overarching vision when advising you on your best course of action.

Create

To live means spending money, even if that is only on food and shelter. Most people's lifestyle is greater than this, and people often have several bank accounts for different purposes, but it seems that many people do not make or stick to a budget. Mastering this financial discipline may be particularly challenging for our young adults, but at the very least they should track spending, if only to emphasise that everyone should spend less than they receive. One thing is certain: they will need strategies to help them to control their spending.

Living costs

Living costs vary, depending upon lifestyle, needs, desires, and region. There are certain classes of expenses that everyone has in common, while other expenses are more discretionary and likely to depend on circumstances. The following illustration is just an example designed to stimulate thought on different categories of spending. Of course, if your child is in a supported living environment, many of these expenses will already be covered.

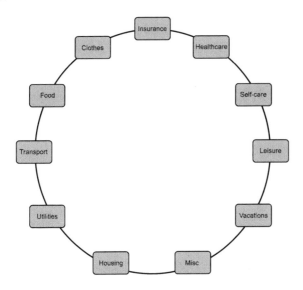

Examples of some common living expenses

For the expense categories that you intend your child to control, there needs to be a plan about how these will be paid. Automated payments are a good option for many, but we also need to devise a system to ensure that the money allocated is not spent elsewhere before payment is made.

You may decide to instigate a system of different bank accounts to organise spending, or discrete pots within a single account. This might be a holding account for fixed costs that can be automated, and separate accounts for more discretionary spending so that when the money is spent, it is spent. This can ensure that the major payments are covered, but having separate bank accounts for different aspects of spending does not in itself prevent overspending. To try to do that we must talk about tracking spending and delayed gratification.

Tracking spending

Some people will set budgets for their spending, but the truth is that many people find it hard, not only to make a budget but then to stick to it. Given this, you should not be unrealistic in your expectations for your child. Rather than try to maintain a budget, you could try replacing it with a system of tracking spending. This is less complicated but still provides them with information about where they spend their money.

Many people only have a vague idea of where they spend their money. Sometimes they get into debt for no other reason than this. Debt is certainly one thing our young adults should avoid. Apart from the extra expense of interest payments, it is often hard to pay off debt; we know from the media, if not from personal experience, what can happen when things then spiral.

A spending tracker monitors the amount spent on each category every month. Bank apps tend to have a tracking facility built-in, so much of the record-keeping is already done. By using a spending tracker, they can analyse their spending and see where their money goes. This then enables them to pose questions such as whether they are overpaying for a particular utility, or if their spending on a particular category is excessive. It is only when our young people start to track their outgoings that they have the information they need to start to think about their spending habits.

Delayed gratification

Delayed gratification is all about waiting for a certain time to pass before we buy something, rather than spending on impulse. Personal finance experts often advise that, if you want something, you should wait twenty-four hours before buying it. The logic behind this is that you have time to reflect on whether you *really* want to buy the thing, whether you can afford it, whether you actually need it, whether it can be bought more cheaply, and so on, rather than simply acting unthinkingly just because you want it. By imposing a twenty-four-hour rule on yourself, you are creating a barrier to impulsive spending.

The discussion you have with your child around delayed gratification is entirely up to you. You might agree that you will always go back the following day to buy it if they still want it; if online, you may agree to wait twenty-four hours. When shopping with my daughter and she sees something she wants to buy, I have sometimes asked her whether she really wants it or whether that money would be better saved for when we are on holiday. This is not saying no to spending, it is simply offering an attractive alternative that she can easily picture in her mind – ice-creams in the sun or souvenir shopping. Sometimes the shop purchase still wins, but often she will choose to keep her money for things she knows she enjoys.

The point of delayed gratification is not to stop spending, but to wait a certain amount of time before deciding. It should not be used as a trick to stop spending, but simply as a tool to ensure that spending is mindful, conscious, and justified. Our hope is that they realise they do not need something quite as much as they first thought.

DANA'S STORY

Dana's mother understands that some of Dana's lack of money sense is due to her age, but she is also aware that Dana needs to start taking on more responsibility as she grows. Because Dana's mother lives on a single income, she is used to managing money. She believes the best way for her daughter to start increasing her financial understanding is through the use of separate bank accounts.

She helps Dana set up several bank accounts for different categories of spending. In her main account, she gets her state benefit. From this account, regular automated payments are made to her other bank accounts, and payments are made for her phone contract and the small amount her mother charges her for rent. Her mother wants her to see these as regular monthly expenses.

She also has an account for leisure, where a specific amount goes each week. Other accounts include a toiletries account, a hairdressing account, and a clothes account. These accounts are not always used each month.

Every Sunday night, Dana's mother sits down with Dana and uses a simple spreadsheet to help her track her spending. She takes the totals from her banking apps and enters them into her spreadsheet under the relevant category. This enables her to see how much she has spent in each category that week.

Dana's mother plans to add more accounts only when Dana can manage this without help. Dana's mother believes that by building this habit of tracking her spending, Dana will develop better financial literacy. Although it is only early days, already there are signs that it may be working.

Actions for Create

Create is about organising the systems that will control your child's money. It might also mean teaching rules of thumb to live by, for example, practising delayed gratification or tracking their spending.

For you, Create might mean death tax planning, and taking the time to go to the lawyer's office to sign your will and set up powers of attorney. If applicable, it would include appointing future trustees or setting up a guardianship. Ask yourself when you are going to do this, and if not now, why not?

The basic rules that govern personal finances are the same for everyone. Everyone must pay out less than they receive, whether that be through salary, benefits, or a combination. One way to ensure this balance is correct and to ensure they have sufficient money to make the necessary payments is to divide what they need to spend into categories, and then use automation and separate accounts to pay for different items. It may be that they will never fully grasp all the concepts of money management and personal finance, but they wouldn't be alone in this. What is beyond doubt, however, is that they will need a certain amount of money sense if they are to live more independently, and that controlling spending is the absolute key to financial security.

Assess

Everyone should review their financial affairs from time to time. With your child, you should note their spending habits. If a trust deals with most of the spending, then it is only a matter of assessing how the trust is managed (which is beyond the scope of this book). However, if we intend to leave them with as much financial control over their lives as possible, this means they need to learn to balance their spending against their income. We should assess this based on their income now, but it's also important to think about what their income might be in the future.

Spending habits

As time passes and they learn whatever system you have put into place, it then becomes time to evaluate how disciplined they are. How ingrained is the habit of tracking their spending? Do they practise delayed gratification techniques when it comes to impulse purchases? Are they regularly managing to balance their spending against income? Are their financial affairs looking healthy overall?

If their spending habits are not working, we should ask ourselves why. Is it that they simply need more time and to be more mature? If this is the case, it may be that another year or two is needed before a proper assessment of their financial habits can be made.

Consider the financial procedures that you have put in place. Are they working as they should? Does your child understand the systems? Are the strategies and techniques working for them? With spending tracking, it may be that the habit cue needs to be made stronger; perhaps a time cue would work better? With my daughter, we do our spending tracking at the same time every week, regardless of anything else. This rigidity sets it in stone as a routine and this quickly then becomes a habit. Also think about whether the reward might need changing. For some people, the feeling of control over their own money is enough of a reward, as it is for my daughter, but others might need something more tangible.

If there are issues with impulse spending, is this a regular problem? We all fall for impulse purchases from time to time, but most of us understand that we cannot have everything we want in life immediately or all of the time. What more can you do to encourage delayed gratification? This might at times involve letting them spend their money unwisely, so they learn from their mistakes when they run out for the week or month. Experience can be the strongest teacher.

What should happen next?

It is unlikely that you will give them total control over all their finances in one go. If you have started small, with say leisure spending, then it may be time to hand over a second category, perhaps clothes.

Separate accounts help compartmentalise different categories of spending. Then maybe they pay for their phone contract, and next you might ask them to pay rent as a way of showing them that housing costs are a significant regular monthly expense. It is a matter of assessing their success each time as you hand over slightly more control of their finances for them to manage themselves.

Assessing what happens next should also apply to your own financial affairs. If you plan on setting up a trust, you should start researching that now. Have you made a will? Have you set up an inheritance plan? Have you got lasting powers of attorney in case something should happen to you? Have you organised your financial affairs so that they are as straightforward as possible? As an incidental, have you also made your funeral wishes known to your family to ease the stress on them as much as possible? While these might be difficult conversations, these tasks are always best done early and in a considered and careful manner. Don't wait for a crisis or emergency to force your hand.

Income assessment

Financial security depends on income. We should consider whether they will have enough by comparing their income to their expenses. We need to understand where their income will come from, now and in the future. Do they have a regular income?

If not, what can be done to change this? If paid work is not an option, what government benefits are currently available? This may mean research to identify what your child qualifies for now and might qualify for in the future. Remember that the system is likely to change under successive governments so this income cannot be exactly calculated nor is it guaranteed, but you can make a best guess based on information currently available.

Just as important is to think through their expenses. Remember to include all their expenses, not just the regular or fixed monthly ones; include variable expenses like holidays, gifts, home expenses, and everything else that doesn't occur regularly. It is sensible to include some contingency funds to account for the unexpected.

How our young adults will be able to afford to live when we are no longer around to support them is one of the biggest concerns for most parents. It is the difference between the life we desire for them and the life we most fear. Knowing they have enough income and that this is balanced against their expenses is financial security for them and peace of mind for us.

RYAN'S STORY

After his voluntary work shifts, Ryan has taken to walking home by himself. With greater independence comes greater freedom, and he likes to look in the window of one particular shop on the way home. Like most people, Ryan wants what he sees. He notices a rather expensive collectable action figure in the shop that he doesn't yet have so he goes in to buy it.

When Ryan arrives home, his parents are disappointed. With money being tight, they thought he understood he needed to cut down his spending. They are annoyed because action figures already fill his room, but they also realise it's just a matter of time before he buys another, and another. They need to assess what they have taught him about money and sensible spending, but how?

They decide to connect the conversation to one of his favourite treats – attending the football. His dad used to take him but is not now well enough. His older brother has promised to take him, but he doesn't have the money to pay for them both. Ryan will need to buy his own ticket, which means he must save money elsewhere if he is to afford it.

When they explain this, Ryan doesn't seem to understand, but the next day he arrives home and proudly announces, 'I walked past the shop today and didn't stop.'

His parents build on this. They know that with greater freedom he will sometimes make choices they disagree with, or do things they don't always want him to do, but that's the price they must pay. He either stays dependent or learns to do more for himself, and with their health problems and their age, they'd much rather the second option. One day Ryan will have to live without them. Better he practises now and makes mistakes, while they're still around to support him. They're pleased with the progress they see so far, and Ryan has already saved enough to attend the football twice.

Actions for Assess

The financial section of a life plan should be assessed regularly. Unlike many of the other things in the life plans for our children, finances have an objective measure. The numbers are either positive or negative. While the negative cannot always be avoided, knowing about it will mean that we can think about steps to change the situation.

Assessing your child's income and expenses should be done regularly. Future income sources and expenses should also be projected to evaluate whether our young adults will be able to afford to live the life they want and that we desire for them. Unless complete control rests with you, they will need to develop certain money skills. Being able to adhere to spending limits is one, not impulsively spending is another. Ideally, they will also learn to track their spending and have some measure of control over their financial health.

Assessment should happen regularly to make sure they are gradually building up a stable future. Einstein was reputed to have said, 'Compound interest is the eighth wonder of the world. He who understands it, earns it; he who doesn't, pays it.' Whether or not this came from Einstein, it is indeed true that small amounts of money invested over a long time usually add up to a significantly larger sum than was originally invested. This is how pensions, workplace retirement plans, and other investment schemes work, and it's something we should keep in mind when considering when to start preparing financially for our child's future.

It is also important to regularly evaluate our own finances and consider how they impact our children. Even if finance is not your favourite subject, for peace of mind it is worth spending time thinking about it regularly and ensuring things are as healthy and organised as they can be, whatever your financial situation.

Legacy

Understanding Legacy on the Financial line can be confusing. Even if you don't consider yourself well off, you can still leave a significant financial legacy because it's not the money you leave them, but rather it's their relationship to money and the organisation of their finances. Everyone has money come into their lives and we all make choices about how that money is used and spent. Your legacy to them should be instilling good money habits.

In a practical sense, leaving a good financial legacy means that your child will follow certain habits (rules) about the spending of money, and understand from which bank account it is spent. It might also be a connection to and willingness to learn from a money mentor, possibly a trustee if they have a trust. Because money is such an abstract concept, it's important to rely on spending habits. Included in this might be rules about delayed gratification that are so ingrained that they are an automatic habit. The key thing is a sound system of financial organisation that leaves them enough to live on, even if it doesn't cover all they desire.

You might find that teaching stops along the Financial line is one of the more frustrating things you can do with your child. It is certainly one of the most challenging, and you may at times feel that money management is a skill they will simply never grasp – and they wouldn't be alone. It is important to remember, however, that just because something is hard is not a reason not to persevere with it. Leaving them with no money skills whatsoever would be a recipe for disaster if other checks and balances aren't put in place, so try to keep chipping away at these stops regularly.

Your financial legacy can never be considered complete until you have all your financial affairs organised. This includes gradually separating your finances away from theirs, and it may involve inheritance planning. This could mean discussing your will with others, perhaps their siblings, to ensure they understand your thinking behind it and the decisions you have made. You may need to decide on future trustees or identify who will advise them on financial matters. It may be as simple as just letting them know who to turn to if they have problems with bills and getting things done from a practical living perspective. It is important to ensure they understand who they should and shouldn't trust when it comes to talking about financial affairs.

A solid life plan, that you have been working on throughout this book, will enable you to share your thoughts with others about what would be a good life for your child. You want others to understand your wishes and desires for your child, and ensure they are carried out even when you are not around. Your plan must be totally clear because not everyone has your great imagination nor your determination to ensure your child lives a fully rewarding and fulfilling life. Whether or not your child will be able to have this life will depend, to a large extent, on their finances. Give yourself this peace of mind: write a life plan and share it with those people who will support your child in the future, especially those people who will advise them on money, because the success of your plan will fall to them once you are no longer around. Ensuring this longevity is another aspect of your financial legacy to your child.

OUR STORY: Establishing a trust

From when she was very young, I always questioned whether I should set up a trust for my daughter. I remained a little reticent because, like many of us, trusts were things I'd heard about only in relation to very wealthy people, and I didn't have any personal experience. The language around trusts is also confusing and I didn't know where to start, so although it was always at the back of my mind, it took a long time before I acted on it.

A few years ago, I finally took the plunge and set up a trust. Although I thought by then I was familiar with trusts, it is only since setting one up that I've truly come to understand some of the advantages they have for my daughter. Whatever the trust holds is regarded as separate from her finances so she would always be eligible for means-tested government benefits. Trusts also act as a safeguarding mechanism: for example, if someone were to befriend her and after gaining her trust, requested a loan of a large amount of money, the trustees would be able to intervene and if necessary prevent it.

I have also found that a trust lasts a lot longer than I thought, so after my daughter dies, any remaining funds in it will be passed to our family in general. This means that whatever I leave, providing the trustees do a good job managing it, will eventually benefit my great grandchildren that I may never meet.

The hardest thing about setting up a trust, I've found, is choosing future trustees. Trustees are the ones who control the money and assets in a trust. If they don't know how to manage money, one can only imagine how the trust will fare. I hope I've chosen wisely.

The thing the trust gives me, though, is peace of mind. I can leave money to it in my will and feel reassured my daughter will be financially secure, safe from herself and safe from others who might seek to take advantage of her. My goal is to ensure she always has enough money to live the life she wants. I want to do that in a way that gives her the greatest degree of independence while also ensuring the greatest financial security.

The Financial line in context

When our children are born, their finances are totally entwined with ours. We pay for everything they need, from clothes to shelter, from healthcare needs to entertainment. There will, however, come a point when we need to realise that their finances cannot be tied to ours forever. We must make an active decision to separate our financial affairs from theirs before the tie gets forcibly cut, which could be very messy if left to chance. Without a planned transition to separate finances, there will be no organisation and no training for them on how to manage their money.

A life plan will enable us to face the reality of this situation. The best safeguard for financial security is to ensure their ability to manage money themselves, but this is not always possible, in which case a guardianship or trust might be the solution. We should then use our life plan to determine which other stops need to be in their route map and how these will be addressed. Their life plan must include long-term answers about how their financial affairs will be managed.

If they are to control some or much of their financial affairs, how will this relate to the other lines in their life plan? Organising bank accounts is a personal management skill from the Daily Living line and needs a reliance on habit to ensure it's done effectively. Speaking to people to find out about bills or to query payments is a Relationships line skill.

The Financial line is slightly different from the other lines in that so much of it is within your direct control. The more deeply you plan and organise it, the greater the beneficial effect. The thing that sometimes stops people thinking about this, however, is that it relies on us thinking about our mortality. We need to make decisions about how their finances will work long after we have died, and we also need to make plans for our own finances in our will. This can be difficult.

A life plan will enable your child to live their best life. Time has been taken to plan and prioritise what's important for them, to consider what will give them a happy life, what will give them a sense of purpose and meaning, what will give them pride and self-respect, and what will give them a greater feeling of being independent, autonomous people.

Given all that, why would you let all this fail because the Financial line hasn't been adequately planned? You wouldn't! We have to face reality. Not everyone can leave large assets, but everyone can leave a significant legacy in terms of sound financial organisation. Don't feel guilty about what you leave financially – a considered and well-structured financial system and basic understanding are far more valuable. They will receive money from somewhere, if only from government benefits. How that is used and organised depends to a large part on you and the work you do with your child, now and in planning for their future.

Conclusion

L ike all parents, you want the best for your child. At times, I suspect you have found life as a parent to a child with additional needs to be challenging. It can seem like you are fighting against a system that, while apparently designed to support you, often seems unable to adapt and support you and your child. The world can seem inflexible and unforgiving, and your child has perhaps occasionally even seemed adrift, constantly swimming against the tide. Now imagine that future, and a world without you there by your child to throw them a life ring…

This is why you need to make a life plan for your child. You need to outline what is important to you and your child and then lay down some guidelines about how those things are to be achieved. The key concepts of this plan, as outlined in this book, are simple. Divide your child's life up into the four lines of the Red Giraffe Route Map:

1. Daily Living

2. Relationships

3. Purpose

4. Financial

You next need to think about the various stops on each of these four lines, consider which of them might be appropriate for your child, and then what they will need to do to be able to navigate each stop successfully. This is, in essence, the substance of their life plan.

To develop their life plan further, use the VOCAL Method. That means you need to have a Vision for each aspect of their life, decide on the best Options, Create a plan to take them there, and after a while Assess whether the plan will work to deliver the vision.

If you work through this process systematically and carefully, you will eventually be able to conceive and deliver your Legacy – your gift for your child's future. Speed of implementation is not as important as consistency, but key to everything is regular assessments, to appraise, refocus, and even redirect or modify if required to ensure success. A well-structured and happy life is beyond doubt the greatest gift you can leave your child, but the real prize is the benefits it will bring them as they develop greater independence, increased self-respect and a heightened sense of self-worth. They will become the best that they can be, and you will also benefit from peace of mind, confident that you can now answer the question of what happens when you are no longer around.

You are the expert on your child, but you will need to use your imagination to help them reach their full potential. Push yourself to dream confidently and optimistically, and then put the stops in place to bring this vision to reality. High ambitions and expectations for them will mean they will learn to do more for themselves. They will grow and mature, and with that, their relationship with you will change. You need to presume they will have a purpose to their day after full-time education finishes and take all the necessary steps to make this happen. You need to plan for a time when your life and finances become separated from theirs so that they can one day live without you. These can be difficult things to think about, but far worse is the danger if they are not thought through adequately and in a timely manner. You need to plan for your child's future now, and that means also planning for your own future, and for the time when you are gone.

You have already taken the first steps towards this planned future by reading this book, but this book is worth nothing, and your time reading has been wasted, if you don't act. Knowledge without action is pointless. Far better less knowledge implemented well, than all the knowledge in the world sitting on a bookshelf. There is no point in having the most wonderful vision of your child's future if you take that knowledge with you to the grave – you need to lay that plan down, share it with those who matter, and take the necessary steps towards making that vision a reality. You don't need to have all the answers to start your journey, but you need to start the journey if you are to find the answers.

I am a parent myself, and I am all too familiar with long sleepless nights worrying about my child's future. However, much as I empathise, my enthusiasm for, and conviction in, the importance of a life plan is not so much for you but for your child. I've faced many of the situations you have as a parent, and it's always been my conviction that my daughter was so much more capable than others seemed to believe, so I needed to build a solid foundation from which she could explore an expanded world. I am sure you think the same about your child otherwise you wouldn't have taken the time to read this book, and for that I thank you. We have always been our children's strongest advocates, and although our role changes as they grow, we will always be their cheerleaders and most devoted fans. The echoes of our cheers will continue to be heard by our children long after we have gone if we leave them a legacy of self-worth, increased independence and confidence, and a belief in their value to the world. I hope this book will help you to do this.

I would love to hear about your journey, so please connect with me. Being the parent to a child with additional needs is tough. We love them, but it's made us face challenges beyond our expectations, and at times most of us have probably doubted whether we'd have the strength or perseverance to get through. We are better people for what our children have shown us, and each day I learn a little more from my daughter's journey in the world.

After everything has been said, what is most important is the legacy you leave to your child. Your legacy to your child isn't money, it's the things you teach them; the things you believe in; the things that matter to you and your child; the love; the memories. It's the personal values you instil in them – *the way you do things in your family*. It's what you believe is the right way to live. What they will look back on is the time they spent with you and the ways you showed them how to live. Your legacy is their future – let's make that their best life.

References

Caldow, Debra, *Expanding Worlds* podcast, www.expandingworlds.com, accessed July 2023

Duhigg, Charles, *The Power of Habit: Why we do what we do, and how to change* (Random House Books, 2014)

Fogg, BJ, *Tiny Habits: Why starting small makes lasting change easy* (Penguin Books, 2020)

Gladwell, Malcolm, *Outliers: The story of success* (Penguin Books, 2009)

Gray, Carol, 'Social Stories', www.carolgraysocialstories.com, accessed July 2023

Hyatt, Michael and Harkavy, Daniel, *Living Forward: A proven plan to stop drifting and get the life you want* (Baker Books, 2016)

Ziglar, Zig, *Developing the Qualities of Success: How to stay motivated* (Made for Success Publishing, 2014)

Acknowledgements

Without the following people, this book would never have made it to press.

I am indebted. Thank you all.

Tracy Busby, Debra Caldow, Siobhan Costello, Scarlett Ford, Victoria Garrard, Joe Gregory, Sarah Hetherington, Camilla Johnson, Lucy Lloyd-Price, Hannah Loach, Lucy McCarraher, Grace Rojo, Lynne Saunders, Bernadette M Schwerdt, Jasper Steinhausen, and Gordon Tillman.

The Author

Graham Caldow lives with his wife Debra and youngest daughter in the south of England. As a teenager, he sought adventure and travelled overland through Iran to India. Later, he saw mountain gorillas in Zaire, viewed glaciers off the southern coast of Argentina, and marvelled at the statues on Easter Island. His focus changed with the birth of his second daughter, and now one of his major life goals is to ensure she consolidates her independence skills to ensure she will thrive even when he is no longer around to support her. He reads with her each night, and she believes he is much improved under her guidance. Red has become his favourite colour.

Giraffes have been forced upon him. He likes to take long walks by the beach each day to wash clutter out of his mind and pay lip service to exercise. Paradise for him would still be a sandy beach in a hot country with a good book, interesting food, and friendly people, but now with Debra by his side and his two girls. Before he dies, he would love to take a trip into space to orbit the Earth and experience zero gravity.

🌐 www.whatspossibleplan.com

💼 www.linkedin.com/in/grahamcaldow

📷 @grahamcaldow